# From A Maze to Amazing

## A guide to setting up your first business

Dr Terri Bourne

www.terribourne.com



ISBN 9798717163583

Cover design by Lucy Green

Also by Dr Terri Bourne

The Beginning of the End: A practical guide to retirement preparation for the small business owner

# Table of Contents

*"All our dreams can come true if we have the courage to pursue them."*

*Walt Disney*

# Introduction

If you are thinking of setting up your own business this book is your starting point. Many of us think we have an idea that would make a great business but have no information about where to start or what running a business would be like.

There are a million and one questions to answer when starting out in your first business. It might all seem like you are in the middle of a maze when thinking about what you need to do to get started. Every turn you make seems to lead to a dead end, going down avenues you have tried before, confusion and anxiety. Like being in a maze, you know that there will be a way through it but at the moment you feel a little bit lost. This book will help you through the maze of starting and setting up your own business.

I know the way through; having set up 7 different businesses in a total of 20 different locations, I have a blueprint. If you follow me, I'll get you out onto the other side and you will emerge from the labyrinth of routes with a better understanding of where you need to focus your attention in order to start your business, with a clear plan of what to do next.

This book is a comprehensive guide for the complete beginner. Or if you've already started your business but feel a bit lost, it will help steer you through, putting everything in place to ensure the smooth running of your venture. And if you are a first-time entrepreneur, welcome to the wonderful world of entrepreneurship, where you can take an idea, turn it into reality and make some money along the way.

From a Maze to Amazing will help you decide if running your first business is an option, and if it is, exactly how you can go about setting it up. By putting everything in place in an organized way, you can concentrate on the business and not on the paperwork.

I have tried to think of everything and although this may seem a little overwhelming at the moment, I am a great believer in understanding and implementing when you are ready and not before. Having been in business for over twenty years, I am now able to share the knowledge gained from all this experience. Over the years I have had concepts and ideas explained to me but if I wasn't ready, I didn't get it. This could be you. Don't worry if it all seems like a lot of information. You will process what you need now, and the rest is here for when you are ready.

**What Can I Expect?**

We begin the book by looking at the suitability of your business idea and your suitability as a business owner. If there is any doubt that your business will not work, you will find out in the first chapter. It may then be back to the drawing board for you. If that happens, don't worry. It doesn't mean that you will never run your own business, it just means that either you or your business idea are not ready yet. Better to find out now, one chapter into a book than spend lots of time, money and effort on chasing an idea that won't work.

However, if your idea is good and you feel ready to go, you can start planning your business, including the finances, branding and marketing, premises, paperwork and finally, whether you will need to take on other people.

The book is set out into 7 chapters, each one a complete resource for you to think about and put ideas and systems in place that work, if you choose to adopt them. Everything that we talk about in this book has been tested over the years in one business or another. It has been tweaked to make it the easiest and simplest way of doing things. You have the benefit of over 20 years business experience along with all the mistakes that I have learned from. I'm not saying that you won't make mistakes of your own. I truly believe that by making mistakes you learn a lot, but when reading through this book, I will be holding your hand so you make fewer mistakes and can therefore concentrate on setting up and running your new business.

Throughout the book you will find useful tips that can be taken as individual nuggets, or which may relate directly to the specific chapter. In addition, and to take your thinking further, I have included **Something To Think About** into most chapters to get you thinking about a specific issue. During the course of the book you will find stories and case studies with examples from my own experience and that of others. Within each chapter you will also find 'calls to action', called **On Your Own**, making sure your business progresses with each chapter. At the end of each chapter there is a brief summary, the **Chapter Takeaways**, accompanied by further calls to action, so you can quickly look back at what has been discussed and have some starting points for your next move.

Don't worry if this takes some time, there's no rush. It's better to understand properly what you have to do and put actions into place as you go along, rather than overwhelm yourself with too much to do. If this happens you may not start or do anything. And finally, if you feel that any of the chapters are not relevant to you then move on. Come back to them when you are ready.

*"When you find an idea that you just can't stop thinking about, that's probably a good one to pursue."*

*Josh James, co-founder and CEO of Omniture and Domo*

# Chapter One: Suitability

In this chapter we look at the concept of suitability. Two main areas are covered, firstly your suitability as a person to run a business, moving on to whether your business idea is suitable to sustain a business. If you are not ready to start your own business for any reason it will show up here. By starting here, you will know if your idea is a good one and whether you are the right person to implement it.

If you find that your idea won't work or that you are not the right person for it, don't be disheartened. It is better to find out now, right at the beginning, rather than put a lot of effort, time and money into an idea that possibly won't work. If this is the case, you may have other ideas worth pursuing in the future, so all is not lost. Only you can make the decision to go forward, so you will need to be honest with yourself about your own suitability.

## Personal Suitability

### Your reason why

Why do you want to run your own business? What is it that has brought you to this book? Did you buy it yourself or has someone spotted something entrepreneurial in you and given it to you as a gift?

Lots of people think they can start their own business. They have an idea to make or do something differently and 'hey presto' the talk is all about setting it up and running it. The reality, however, is that people rarely follow it through. There is a difference between having a great business idea and having a great business and for most people the idea is where it all stops.

Some questions for you;
• Why do you think you could be any different?
• Do you have a yearning to get out of the rat race or your day job?
• Do you daydream about all the free time that running your own business will give you, more time to spend with your family, for example?

If you think that starting and running your own business will give you time, you need to reassess. If you think that it will be easier than your current job, think again. Having a business is hard work. In years to come you may be able to have more time but certainly at the beginning, which is your current place, it is a long, hard graft. But the rewards can be worth it.

**Childhood entrepreneur**

Some business owners tell stories of being childhood entrepreneurs. I used to run a disco from a friend's garage. My dad had an old record player and some records from the sixties. I charged an entrance fee for local children to attend, so perhaps I was always destined to run my own business.

Does entrepreneurship run in the family? Are you from a family of business owners? I did some research a few years ago, interviewing 10 entrepreneurs. Initially, only one of them said that they were from a business background, until we dug a bit deeper and they remembered shops that grandparents had run, business side-lines that their mum used to do part time to earn a little extra, or a brother who bought and sold things at a profit. There are many ways to come from a business background.

Do you know someone who is an entrepreneur? A family member or a friend? Is that why you are thinking of starting your own business? When most people are asked to name an entrepreneur, they usually come up with someone famous and often Richard Branson is a favourite. Entrepreneurs, business owners and the self-employed come in many shapes and sizes. For me, an entrepreneur is someone who generates a business idea and then sees it through to fruition by starting a business; after it is set up, they may or may not be the one who runs it. A business owner is the person who owns the business, sometimes, but not always, running it as well. A self-employed person works for themselves, sometimes employing others. Often in the above examples, the label someone is given depends on their involvement in the business.

An entrepreneur can start, set up and run a business or buy a going concern and continue to run it. I think the difference between the word business owner and entrepreneur is creativity. The entrepreneur is able to take an idea from inception and make it into a business. Are you an entrepreneur? Is this what you want to be? Is this how you want to work?

**TIP**
From now - anything you do should be to help your business move forward.

**Your motivation**

People think that being a business owner can give you time, status and money. Yes it can, but not necessarily all of them, not necessarily in that order and maybe not as much of each as you would like. Working for yourself is hard work. It's also a little bit scary as you are totally responsible for your income, and in some cases, the income of others. It can be stressful working under this kind of pressure and although you may have gone into self-employment to get a bit of extra time, the reality is that you need to work in order to get paid, however you are feeling or whatever else is going on in your life.

It is a misconception that working for yourself allows you more free time, certainly not at the beginning when everything is new for you. The only good thing is that it doesn't *feel* like you are working more hours, often because you are enjoying yourself and enjoying the learning, time goes quicker, and it doesn't seem like work.

You do, however, need stamina. You also need drive. No-one will be telling you to get up and go out to work when you work for yourself. That's your job, so you need a lot of self-discipline. You need to be an organized person or use tools to help you become one. You will need to be a planner.

You have to be good at maths, or at least have a basic grasp, so you can get your numbers right. Although this is an area you can outsource, I would strongly recommend, if it is a weak area of yours, that you train yourself up so you understand what is going on with the numbers. Later and throughout the book, there are recommended systems which you can put in place, all to help you make your business run smoothly.

**Myth vs Reality**

Entrepreneurs and business owners come in all personality types. You don't have to have shed loads of confidence (contrary to popular belief), and you don't have to be an extrovert. You have to be you, with a business idea that will work.

Later on, we discuss branding and how that fits in with your values and how you want to run a business. A myth perpetuated by the media is that all entrepreneurs are extrovert, confident people. You will need some confidence, particularly if you are selling a product or service – and this covers most businesses but, depending on your personality and comfort zone, there are ways of doing something that might best suit your personality.

Another myth is that entrepreneurs are born lucky. For most people this is untrue. Many famous entrepreneurs started out in life from modest backgrounds and their friends and connections have nothing to do with the scale of business that they have managed to grow.

*"I'm a great believer in luck, and I find the harder I work, the more I have of it."*

*Thomas Jefferson, US Founding Father and President*

Now, there is some truth in that!

More questions;
- Who are your role models?
- Who do you look to and think, "I want to be like them?"
- What are your reasons for that?
- What have they got, or do they do that you admire?
- How can you adapt that to your own life?
- Is it your wish to be a role model to someone else?
- Are you already a role model?
- What will other people be able to say about you and your business to carry them and their
  business forward?

**What is suitability in your business?**
I cannot know what type of business or industry you are thinking of going into so I will have to be a bit general here. In some industries there is a definite protocol for suitability. Let's say that you have a criminal conviction for something in the past. You are still obliged to declare this, even if it is 'spent' in some cases, for some industries. Of course, you will be running your own business, but the first place to sort out your suitability checks are with yourself.

It would be very disappointing to find out that you had set your heart on something, only to find out that in that industry, as the owner or person directly responsible, you were not suitable to run the business. There are ways to mitigate against this of course, perhaps by employing someone who is prepared to be the front person, but unless this person is your business partner, you may find that giving that kind of control to someone else so early in your business career is not what you want to do.

In the next chapter we discuss what kind of entity your business will be, for example, a limited company or another type of business structure. Depending on what you choose, depends to some extent on your suitability. As a Company Director you will have to abide by a few 'rules' including ones that are about your previous financial status (on a personal and business level). If, for example, you have been bankrupt or insolvent, this may affect the kind of business you are allowed to set up.

You will need to spend time looking at your own suitability and of those who you need to work with in your new business set up. Again, if you need to employ people to do what you can't or are not allowed, then expect costs to be higher than if you can set up this business by yourself.

Most people choose to run businesses related to what they already know, and this may come from already working for a company. When you work as an employee you are gaining skills all the time to help you to do the job which benefits your employer. In addition, those skills are building up for your personal benefit. Lots of skills are transferable and this, of course, relates to working for yourself. You probably have many of the skills you require for your business if you have been employed. For example, working in or heading up a team, dealing with people, customer relations, working with certain computer programs and systems, computational and linguistic skills and having confidence to speak to people on the telephone, via email or in person. All these are transferable skills that you can take with you when the time is right.

**Qualifications - do you have them or do you need to gain them?**

We now turn our attention to qualifications. In your new business are particular qualifications necessary? Have you got them? For some types of business certain qualifications are desirable. In others they are essential. If you are choosing to set up a food outlet for example, you will probably need relevant food hygiene and preparation certificates for workers. As the person in charge, it is also advisable for you to understand your responsibilities as to what has to happen in a commercial kitchen. Or if you were opening a children's day nursery, you would need to make sure that your staff are suitable to work with children from a safeguarding perspective, in addition to being qualified to do so.

Gaining a level of understanding of other people's qualifications will assist you when it comes to working out which employees you need to place where. I must stress however, that you do not have to have all these qualifications yourself. If you employ an accountant to help with your accounts, you would not expect to sort out the accounts yourself, but you probably would understand his or her role and how that could assist you in your business. The same is true of all employees or people helping you in your business.

Gaining a qualification is different, but you do need to think about this now before you start your business. If there is a vital qualification required, is it a good idea to trust that part of the business to someone else? Or are you better waiting until you are qualified before you start on your self-employed journey? These are all things to think about whilst you are considering what is involved in starting your own business.

For your specific business idea, make a list of what qualifications you will need, then decide if it will be you or someone else who will qualify. You will then need to write an action plan to get everything in place, in a timely manner. Don't worry if action plans are new to you, we cover all sorts of planning in the next chapter.

***On Your Own:***
Make a list of qualifications required for your specific business.
Decide if it is you or someone else who will gain them.
Write a time-bound action plan.

**What kind of knowledge is required for your new business?**
We have already touched on you gaining skills while working for someone else. What knowledge areas do you need for your new business? Do you have them? How can you gain them? Nowadays, we go straight to our computers, putting our queries into a search engine for instant results on what it is we need to know. This is a great way to start gaining industry knowledge. But what about what you don't know you don't know?

Only a few decades ago people were recruited and revered for their knowledge and also their experience. Experience is still important; when you train to get a particular qualification, you sometimes have the knowledge of how to do something but not the experience of actually doing it.

It's a bit like someone explaining to you how to make a cup of tea in writing. It all looks fine until you try to do it and find out that a cup could be a mug, or the instructions you got used loose leaf tea and a tea-strainer but you can't find either in the cupboards, only some little bags of brown stuff... You get the idea. Experience of doing something gives a much higher level of understanding and enables you to change what is in front of you based on your knowledge.

Do you have the experience needed or are you looking at buying in the experience for your new business? If you have to buy in the experience it may be expensive in all sorts of ways.

**The cost of lack of experience**
When I was opening a new day nursery for children, I didn't have the experience at the time to run the actual site myself, so I employed someone who had already been a nursery manager. This was a costly exercise for lots of reasons.

Firstly, she had a healthy disregard for finance. It wasn't her money, so she just spent her budget and then asked for more, overpaying continually on items and setting up long term contracts with suppliers which were not in the interest of the company.

Secondly, she wasn't actually very good at her job. This was down to my lack of experience when employing her, I think I put her enthusiasm down to experience, yet she did not manage to bring in more customers and extend the provision.

Lastly, in her role as manager and on behalf of the company, she employed her friends, who were just as mediocre as she was. She was able to do all this as I had not got the experience of running a nursery at the time, to recognise what she was doing.

I could see that it wasn't working for me or my business, so I spent a year retraining and getting the experience I needed by working for friendly competitors out of the area. They were very happy to have me on board for my qualifications and business experience and I was gaining a valuable insight into how to actually run a nursery myself. Within a year I was able to take over as the manager. My own nursery was on its knees, due to this manager not understanding how business works and what business owners have to be continually mindful of. When it is your own business you need to look at how to manage the finances as best you can, as this is where most small businesses fail. We cover finances later in the book.

It may be that you have been working in a similar industry to the one your business is in, so have gained enough experience to set up on your own. If you have to wait until you have the appropriate level of knowledge, qualifications and experience, I strongly suggest you do this.

**Your Business and Work-life Balance**

Many would-be entrepreneurs dream of having more time and a better work-life balance by working for themselves. If you are a parent and can see that running your own business might give you more time at home with your children, and this is your reason for starting a new business, think carefully. The Covid-19 pandemic proved to many that trying to work whilst children are around at home is really difficult.

Is the intended business suitable to work around the home, if that's where you are choosing to run it from? What will happen to your children when you are working? It's not fair on your children to play second fiddle to your business when you are supposed to be with them. And it's not fair on your business to play second fiddle to your children.

It's not easy. You could read a whole book on work-life balance alongside trying to run a business. Almost always there is a compromise. Sometimes you will feel resentful of either the business or your family. Often you will feel guilty. On occasions, no-one gets the best of you as you are spread too thinly.

However, it can be done if you are organized. If you particularly want to do the school run at either end of the day, set up your business from the start to cater for this. You have a golden opportunity now whilst you are in thinking mode.

• How could you structure your day so you can have your cake and eat it?
• What contingencies do you have in place?
• What about holiday times?
• Will the type of business you intend to run need to be open at certain times?

Think about how to structure your ideal day or week and then see if it fits in with your business plans. If not, change it. If certain aspects of work-life balance are important to you, change either the business or your commitments.

Another aspect of work-life balance is *when* you are working. If you are dealing mainly with people in another country or time zone, this will dictate your business hours to some extent. Similarly, if your new business runs mainly at weekends or evenings then these times will be your hours. We are a long way away from a 9-5 culture, unless that is when you want to work.
Hours of business is something to consider carefully right at the beginning of your start up journey. You will need to consider when your customers or clients will want your business to

operate. There's no point in you working 9.30am to 2.30pm term time only, if your customers require the business in the early evenings. These times may suit you, however, if they are not when it is convenient for your customers, you will be setting up your business to fail.

Think about when you should 'open' for business. When are your customers likely to buy? This includes customers who are using the internet. Is all your business going to be automated or do you need to have yourself (or someone else) contactable or as part of a help desk? You may have to research when your customers are likely to buy.

***On Your Own:***
Research when your customers are likely to buy
Decide on the hours you will be 'open'
Work out if this fits in with what you want to achieve.

**The suitability of the business you have chosen**
You have now decided that you are suitable to run your own business but is the business you are thinking about running a suitable one?

**Feasibility and testing the market**
You have an idea in mind so now is the right time to do a feasibility study. This is when you assess if your idea will actually work. It is difficult for me to work that out for you so it is something you will need to do for yourself. Let's take a simple example to show what I mean.

A local market stall sells umbrellas for £9.99 each. They are all black with black handles. Your idea is that your local area could do with brightly coloured umbrellas. You need to test the market and do a feasibility study before you invest in buying a container full of brightly coloured umbrellas to sell.

You buy one or two and go out in the streets when it is raining asking people if they would buy one of your umbrellas and what they think of the colours, what other colours they would want, etc. When you get back you analyse the answers from your research. If most people said that they preferred plain black as it went with all their clothes, then perhaps your business idea would not work in this area. However, if most people said they would definitely buy a new brightly coloured one (they thought that umbrellas only came in black!), then you may have a winning idea. It would be feasible for you to take your idea further.

For an online business you might test the market by running a simple survey to ask people if they would want to use your product or service. However, be warned, people will tick the box that says they think something is a good idea and that they want something in a survey but when it comes to parting with their money, it's a different matter.

We used to run surveys for parents to ask if they wanted an after school childcare service within their schools. Usually, we would get a great response; they all wanted there to be provision within their school. However, when it came to it, they often didn't use the service that was set up as they already had arrangements in place. We had a saying that worked well in our industry for the numbers in survey responses and this was "halve them, then halve them again."

If 80 people said that they desperately needed the service, we would usually end up with only 20 signing up. Once we knew the metrics it was easier to make decisions about whether we set up a new site or not, as we knew we would get about a quarter of the number of people who said that they were desperate for childcare right now.

**TIP**

When putting together a survey, think carefully about the design and questions so that you don't have to go back and ask again!!

**Is there space for your business? Does the market need you?**
When looking at whether the business is suitable you also need to consider whether the market is saturated for your kind of product. If you want to run a nail bar business, for example, how many other nail businesses are there in the area? Is there room for one more or is the area saturated? Is your business going to be so different that it won't matter that there are many others?

It might be worth thinking about running something different or in a different area if there are lots of similar businesses, or do you go down the route of safety in numbers and that you all bring in customers for each other? Take Chinatown for example, where in many large cities this is the area where people go to eat Chinese food because there's plenty of choice.

Just because you have a good business idea does not mean that the market needs it. Getting some idea of the numbers of people who would be interested in your product or service is a good plan before you put lots of time and possible expense into setting it up. You might also need to convince someone else, for example a bank manager, that you have thought about who would use your service or how many of your products you are likely to sell. When you are thinking about this part of your business, make sure you can do a repeatable feasibility study. It could be that your idea works better in a city, or near to the coast or at certain times of the year. It could be that you get a better response to your questions on a certain day, or at a certain time of day, or online.

**What business do you run?**
It is now time to think about what exactly your business will do, who it will be for and how you will run it. The best way to do this is to write an 'Elevator Pitch' for your business. Imagine you are meeting someone (who you want to impress about your business) in a lift or elevator. You have a few floors to travel together and they have just asked you what you do. The idea behind an elevator pitch is that you provide a succinct version of what you are doing and who for, in a short, clear and understandable way; so short, that you can explain it in a few

stops in a lift. It's quite a skill and needs to be written out and then more or less learned so you can say it at any time when required. It will not always be exactly the same, depending on who you are talking to, but you will always cover the same main points.

**The Elevator Pitch**

You need to be really clear about what you offer and how this is different from what everyone else offers. Try different ways of saying things. You don't want to lose them at the beginning. Knowing what 'problem' you are solving for people is a good place to start. However, being too clever or vague about what you are offering will put people off listening to you.

An example of this might be as follows. You sell coloured umbrellas. Rather than just saying this, your opening sentence might be that you brighten up people's rainy days. You then go on to say something about your umbrellas, how they make customers feel even when it's raining. Next you might cover why black traditional ones are no longer the way forward when the world is already a bit drab on a rainy day. You will also need to think about objections before they come up in your elevator pitch. In this case, the listener might say they already have a black one. You can then bring in figures from your feasibility study stating that ??% of people who already had a black umbrella said that they were wanting to buy a brightly coloured one as well. Finally, you will talk about how they can get hold of this valuable commodity.

You may give out a card or a leaflet, talk about a website or shop. I think you get the idea. If someone asked you what you do, you could say "I sell umbrellas online" or you could say something along the lines above. Obviously, you need to go with what is comfortable for you, but the Elevator Pitch gives you a chance to play with your product. It also gives you a sense of fun and turns a normal business exercise into a fun activity. I am a great believer that business should be fun, so I continually look for opportunities to make it so.

***On Your Own:***
Write out your Elevator Pitch and practice saying it to anyone and everyone.

**Your Unique Selling Point**

Do you think you have a unique business idea that no one else has thought about? This could be true, but the chances are it isn't. Ever heard of the phrase 'there's no such thing as a new idea'? Often, when we think we have come up with something different, we investigate it only to find out that it's similar to something already out there. At this point you can go one of two ways. 1. Forget the idea and move on to something that absolutely no one has done, or 2. Go with your idea but make it different enough to attract customers and clients. Your unique selling point, or USP, does just that.

When your business idea is similar to someone else's (and this will be the vast majority of businesses), you need to think about what you are offering and how. Let's take an example to show what I mean. If you are a coach for small business owners, you may have similar qualifications and operate in a similar way to your peers in the coaching industry, so you need to think carefully about what makes you different.

Price points are okay, for example, you could be the cheapest and undercut your peers, but this type of model is not sustainable and may work against you in the long run, as people could assume that the quality isn't there if the price is low. You might be the only business coach in your immediate area, which is a good USP if there are plenty of business owners around your area who need your services. You might combine the coaching with something else, for example, financial planning, which could be what makes you different.

There's lots of ways of looking at this, which can make you seem as if you have the better offer. It probably won't be a huge difference, but you need just enough to set you apart. So, for example, when someone says, 'Why should I come to you instead of the business coach down the road?' you can confidently say what your USP is. For example, we are right here in the city centre, so transport is easy. Or it might be that where you are based, there is ample free parking that could help out your business as well.

Your USP may be connected with what you actually offer, so could be a free consultation or follow up call within one month. Whatever it is, make it easy and cost effective for you, yet seem of value to the client. Buy one get one free, is only sustainable for a short while in most cases. Don't sell yourself short, you will devalue your product or service.

***On Your Own:***
What is your USP?
How is it different from other businesses?

**Time available to work in your business**
We touched on this earlier with regards to work-life balance. Now it's time to look at how much time you can devote to your business. There are several options:

1. Go full time immediately in your new business after reading this book.
2. Go part time in your business, coupled with home commitments.
3. Go part time in your business, keeping paid work (for the moment).

**Go full time immediately in your new business**
This is a leap of faith. It would mean giving up your job, if you have one, and setting up your new business to sustain you financially instead. There are some potential difficulties with this:

a) A new business will take an amount of time to set up. During this time there is a lot to do as you will see as you read through the book. Do you have the time available to commit to the new business?

b) Money may not come in straight away, creating a void in your finances. Do you have a contingency plan for where the money to sustain you will come from? You may have been saving or got

a loan to set up. Is there enough in case it all goes wrong, like a contingency?
c) You don't know if the new business is going to work. If the new business doesn't work out for you then you will have potentially given up your job to start it. You would need to be very sure that you could get another job if it all went wrong or find income from somewhere.
d) As you have never run a business before, it may not be what it seems. You might not like it. If you have given up your job to start your business, you will be in a tricky position if you don't take to running your own business.

**Go part time in your business, coupled with home commitments**

This is similar to the above in that you start to run your business and do this alongside your family commitments. Similar to the work-life balance piece earlier, you will need to be careful that you are organized, so that both your business and family get the best of you, for the sake of yourself and your business.

Women particularly find that setting part time hours for their business works for their family. It may however, slow down the growth of your business for obvious reasons, but if you can live with that you may be able to have the best of both worlds.

**Go part time in your business, keeping paid work (for the moment)**

This may be the way forward if you already have a job or paid work. By working your business around your work commitments, you are able to dip your toes into the world of business. This can be hard work, as you may need to work at weekends and evenings and perhaps during your work holidays, but the rewards can be great. (Remember, when you enjoy what you are doing, it doesn't feel like work.) It gives you an opportunity to 'try before you buy' without giving up your job. This becomes a very secure option and is how many entrepreneurs start their businesses. As with working alongside family commitments, you will need to be very organized and clear on your priorities. If the kind of business you are thinking of setting up will allow you to start it part time whilst keeping your day job, this might be your best option.

**Contingency**

Whichever way you decide to start your business, I suggest you have a contingency plan in place. If you keep paid work for the moment, you will need a contingency for time working on your business. If you decide to share your time between family commitments and your new business, you will need to be organized to fit both in without the guilt. If you give up any paid work, or only work on your business full time you will need a financial contingency to see you through.

***On Your Own:***
Plan for your specific contingencies

**Something to think about:**

**The Rosy Glow of Over-optimism**

We all need to be optimistic when setting up a new business. If we are not, it probably won't even get to the start-up stage. However, entrepreneurs need to be mindful of a tendency to be over-optimistic.

Over-optimism is when someone believes that their business will do substantially better than expected for the norm in that particular field. Over-optimistic entrepreneurs believe they are more likely than others to experience positive outcomes.

Studies on over-optimism have revealed that entrepreneurs have a greater tendency to be over-optimistic than non-entrepreneurs. Even when presented with the facts about potential business failure, some entrepreneurs still believe that their business will be different.

I suppose it starts with the excitement of setting up something new. None of us want to believe that there could be an F word on the horizon (failure). We want our business and our well-planned idea to succeed. Not only that, we want it to do better than our competitors and other businesses in the same field. We can, as entrepreneurs, be a little over-optimistic about what the business can achieve.

Also, your carefully crafted unique selling point (USP) may be instrumental in your optimistic thoughts. Entrepreneurs can become blind-sided to the pitfalls in the excitement of the set up and creation of their new business.

Unfortunately, it's not just the start up stage where over-optimism occurs. Seasoned entrepreneurs also fall into the over-optimistic trap. Most of us think, 'it wouldn't happen to me', and on the balance of probability it might not. Or, 'my idea is completely different or more current' and therefore will work better than the competition. Or 'I shall work harder at sales to bring in more clients, so that my business is more successful than hers.'
Maybe.

I don't want to take away from the excitement of starting your first venture, just to share a little common sense. If you are aware that you could be prone to over-estimating the potential of your new business, it might be enough. You don't need to change your idea; however, you may need to adjust figures for suggested income, turnover, profit or market share. Don't stop dreaming big. Just be aware and think 'how realistic am I being?' Better to start small with success than go large and fail.

**Chapter Takeaways**

We started off by finding out if you are the kind of person who will be able to run your own business. You need to think about your personality, the type of business you want to run, your skills and qualifications, your availability and resources. In addition to you being suitable, you need to assess your business idea and whether it is feasible, whether the business is suitable to run and specifically, for *you* to run it.

**Call to action**

Find out what qualifications and skills are required
Research when your customers are likely to buy
Write your Elevator Pitch
Find your USP
Look at your contingencies.

*"If you fail to plan, you are planning to fail"*

*Benjamin Franklin*

# Chapter Two: Planning

As you are here at chapter two, it must mean you feel you and your business idea are suitable. The real work starts here. If you like planning, this will be your favourite chapter. I cannot stress enough how important it is to develop a plan for yourself and your business. By writing down what you would like to achieve and by when, you will make your business start-up so much easier.

Businesses don't just turn up out of thin air, they need to be carefully thought about and this is what this chapter is all about; from what kind of company structure you want to set up, to what you want to get from a business, to writing your business plan and ongoing plans to propel you forward, concluding with the difference between working *in* and working *on* your business.

**Company Structures**

There are several company structures for you to consider when setting up your business. Below I will outline what I consider to be the advantages and disadvantages of each, at the time of writing. You need to consider both your short and long-term future when setting up your business, for example, if you will be charging VAT (value added tax) for your product. VAT is a business tax set by the Government on the sale of some goods and services. If you register for VAT, you will need to complete a quarterly VAT return.

There are four main types of UK business formations:

<u>Sole trader</u> lots of new businesses set up as sole traders, due to the reduced statutory filing requirements and regulations.

However, the business owner is personally responsible for everything within the business.
As a sole trader you will find:

- Minimum set up
- Minimum administration tasks
- You need to notify HMRC that you are self employed
- No need to register at Companies House
- Your business is not a legal entity so as owner you have complete personal liability for all debts

Limited Company - running a limited company in the UK is one of the most popular ways to run a company. Financial filing is made public, so it is transparent.

Running a limited company you will find:

- It is its own legal entity
- No personal liability for owners or shareholders
- Potential tax advantages of running a ltd company
- You must register the company at Companies House
- All filing information is made public
- All directors and other appointments to the company are public knowledge

Partnership- sometimes called a limited liability partnership or LLP. A minimum of two people are responsible for running the company (the partners). The LLP is run similarly to a limited company. Often LLP's are run by accountants or law firms.

Social Enterprise and not-for-profit companies- are run similarly to limited companies with the emphasis on not-for-profit.

***On Your Own:***
Find out the types of company structures you can set up in your country if you are not in the UK.

When you are considering your company structure, you should look at all the options available to you. If it will just be you to start with, perhaps a sole trader company would be a good place to begin. The scope of this book will not allow me to assist every reader in the right decision but the above will give you an indication of where to start your research. The main thing to remember is that record keeping of all financial transactions is essential.

**Paying the tax due**

Whatever company structure you choose, you will need to keep clear records to make sure you are compliant. No route is easier or less work to do and you will get into hot water if you try to out-do the tax system. Unlike large corporate entities that seem to find ways of reducing their tax liabilities, the smaller companies don't. HMRC are hot on getting in tax money owed to them from small businesses and will make sure you pay your dues. You don't want to owe the tax office lots of money because you have made mistakes. It's best to pay it as you go along, that way it's more manageable.

**Getting a bank account**

Once you have decided on your company name you will need to start getting the ball rolling with several elements, some of which are marketing and branding (covered later), and others are financial, like getting a bank account for your business to operate from.

**Why get a business bank account?**

There are a few reasons why you should get a business bank account:

1. Professionalism – this is very important. If you want to present yourself as a bona-fide company you should register your company (see above) and open a bank account in your business name;
2. Separation – if people put money they owe you for a product or service into your personal bank account it is difficult for you

to know which money is yours and which belongs to your business, which brings me onto;

3. Record Keeping – having a separate bank account means you can keep separate records for all your business transactions. This is important when it comes to informing the tax office how much you have spent on your business and what you have been paid.

When you are ready to get a bank account, think carefully and look at the deals that are on at the time. Some banks offer a period of free banking for new businesses and then a standard monthly rate after that. Will you use cheques? Do you need to pay cash into a branch? Are you able to bank entirely online? If you are, this is usually the cheapest way to bank. Are you the sort of person who likes to meet face to face? If so, having a bank with a designated bank or account manager may be your best option with a local branch to visit. If you need a loan to help you get the business started, you will probably need to apply to a bank manager and therefore will need a business plan. We cover writing a business plan later in this chapter and getting a bank account in more detail in the next chapter.

**What do you want from a business?**

You have decided to start a business. Why are you doing this? What do you want? As discussed in the previous chapter, it is hard work setting up and running a business, so you need to be sure about *why* you are doing it. It's a good idea to write down what you want the business to do for you, that paid employment can't or won't. Your list may include some of the following:

- Freedom from a job
- Responsible for self
- More money
- Greater flexibility
- Better work/life balance
- Less travel
- Independence

***On your own:***
Write your own list for what you want the business to do for you.

When you have completed your list, date it and save it. It will be a great resource to look back on in the future.

**TIP**
Start to keep all your set up ideas. Date them and keep them all in the same place either online or in a journal. It's great fun and very motivating to look back on how you have developed your ideas and grown as a person.

Or do your reasons for wanting to set up a business fall into one of the Big Four?

- Time
- Money
- Status
- Autonomy

*Time* - you may end up with more time from less travel and more effective management of your time. However, you may also find that you take longer to do things than you thought you would, due to lack of experience, making it difficult fitting everything into your available time.

*Money* - if you have come from a regular job, you may need to match that income in your new business to maintain your current lifestyle. You may also hve to take a cut in income, certainly at the beginning of your entrepreneurship journey. Don't expect a bank manager to fund your income. They will need to see a good and solid business plan; they will not be impressed if you want them to fund your current income. You will need to guard against this yourself as well. If you need to borrow to fund your income rather than grow your business, perhaps now is not the right time to be considering setting up your own business, until you have a financial reserve.

*Status* - Do you like the idea of running your own business? Does it hold a certain mystery for you, or a certain status? Some people just like the idea of having their own business. If you are setting up a new business as a status symbol or an accessory, it will probably unravel when you have to work in it and at it. Don't start a business for the wrong reason. When you did the task on your own about what you want from a business, were you honest with yourself? Hopefully, part of that was not just about the status that running your own business can give.

*Autonomy* - being responsible for your own well-being, money and time can be very appealing. Having the space to be yourself and make your own rules, decide on your own timetable and workload can be very attractive. It is also quite daunting to know that you are totally responsible for yourself, and possibly others in time to come.

It is a big decision to start your own business, a huge responsibility towards yourself, your potential employees and your family. Deciding what you are going to do and when you are going to do it is fun, but you should start the business for the right reasons - your reasons. Part of this is clarity - clarity around your purpose and reasons for taking it on. When you know where you are going it's easier to get there.

**Something to think about:**

> *"Begin with the end in mind"*
>
> Stephen Covey author
> The Seven Habits of Highly Effective People

Dr Stephen Covey wrote, 'Begin with the end in mind' as his second habit for highly effective people. In his book, he asks the reader to visualize their own funeral and who will be there and what those people will say about them and their life. In essence, he is asking you to visualize what it is that you want to be remembered for and what would make you proud to hear about yourself.

By looking to the end of a project, you are envisaging exactly where you want to end up, what that looks and feels like. By knowing where you are heading, you will be able to work out the steps along the way which will go towards getting you there - all steps and activities should lead there.

When you are setting up a new business, you should always be looking at the end or where you want the business to be.

Know what your business will look like in the future and work backwards from there. It seems odd to look at the end of the business before you have even started it but there is a good reason for this. You need to know exactly where you are going and which route you are expecting to take. By knowing what you want to achieve, it makes the steps towards getting there much easier to work out.

When you take a taxi you always know where you want to go. You would never get in there and say, "Anywhere please." Similarly, if you caught a plane, you are unlikely to turn up to the airport and say to flight staff, "Surprise me!" You wouldn't know what clothes to take, what language to expect and so on.

Your business journey is no different.

If you know more or less where you are heading, you can plan the best way to get there. If you regard your new business as a journey to plan for, you will find it easier. Let's say in five years' time you expect your business will be turning over £500,000 per year of which 20% is profit, operating from your own premises, employing 5 staff.

For each of these statements you will need to make a plan;

• How will you go from zero to a turnover of £500,000 per year?

• How many customers does that mean, or how many units do you need to sell? Knowing these numbers will help you plan how to achieve your goal.
• Are your customers repeat customers or do you need to find new ones each year and if so, where are these going to come from?
• You may need to plan for having your own premises (and this may take some time.) You may have to do this in stages, for example, renting a small office, to buying something for yourself at a later stage. Again, you will have to plan for this. You cannot just buy premises without considerable thought and planning.
• Employing staff will probably be gradual, unless you need certain skills straight away. It's a big step forward taking on an employee, as you then have a considerable amount of extra responsibility.
• You will have to be confident in your journey to engage the likes of money lenders (if required), potential employees, customers and clients.

Having plans in place for everything will be your security. Later in this chapter we look at which plans to put in place to help you to start and run your own business, and in later chapters we cover some of the above, so don't worry if they are unfamiliar to you at the moment.

**SWOT**

You may have heard of a SWOT analysis. It is a simple tool used in business to identify the strengths, weaknesses, opportunities and threats in your business. It is a simple idea, but it's not easy to do. Traditionally the SWOT sheet is divided into 4 equal squares within a large square, as shown:

| Strengths | Weaknesses |
| --- | --- |
| Threats | Opportunities |

In the box labelled strengths, list all the strengths of your business, or perhaps in your case, your business idea. Next you move onto the weaknesses of the business, then the opportunities your business may give you and finally the threats. You can draw a table, as above, or download one of the many templates on the internet to help you.

**Strengths explained**

It's time for you to think carefully about what your business is offering; what are the benefits? For example, if you want to set up a new online coaching business you may decide that the bespoke diagnostic tool which you have developed for clients is a real strength. Another strength may be that you have been working as a coach in a company for some years, so have lots of experience in this field. From prior working, you may have several positive testimonials from past clients that you can use. You will need to think widely to make sure that you are capturing all the strengths of your business. This information will be particularly useful if you want to request funding at some point. It will also help with your marketing.

**Weaknesses explained**

The next box is for weaknesses. This does not mean personal weaknesses, only the weaknesses of the business. In this box you may write lack of funds to start the business or lack of knowledge in a particular area, no premises at the moment and so on. Within the weaknesses, I always like to think that the problems here are solvable, but maybe not at the moment. For example, the lack of funds is solvable, by getting a bank loan, as is getting the premises, but perhaps not just yet. When you have been in business for some time you will have different weaknesses, but for now you should concentrate on your start-up weaknesses. In the next part of this chapter you will look at action planning to make sure you are able to address the weaknesses.

**Opportunities explained**

In this box write down what opportunities you think there are for your business. For example, you may know that there is no longer a shop selling a particular product in your area but that there is a need for it. It could be that a new housing estate is being built nearby and the people living there will need the services of your new business idea. In the first chapter you learned about over-optimism and this is something to be aware of here. You may need to provide (for yourself and others), actual metrics of the opportunities available. How many people will need your services? Where do they go currently? What makes you sure that they will want to buy from you and that there is a need? It's easy to get carried away with perceived opportunities as you enter your entrepreneurial stage, but you also need to be realistic.

**Threats explained**

The last box is for you to write down any threats to your business. At this stage this could be the threat of redundancy from your day job pushing you to start your business earlier than expected. It could be a competitor who has recently set up locally. It could be that someone has got in there first before you have had a chance to get started. It may be that Government policy has changed so that your business idea is no longer viable.

**A threat to my business**

About ten years ago I set up a childcare voucher company. Parents who used registered childcare could sacrifice part of their salary into a voucher scheme to pay exclusively for childcare. The money was taken at source, so the parent did not pay tax or national insurance on the amount and their employer did not have to pay the tax and national insurance either. Parents got a great saving and our company was paid by the employer out of the savings they were making in tax and NI.

After about 6 years there were already rumblings that the Government was going to scrap the scheme. This was a huge threat to the business. We continued for a little while longer but decided that due to the threat of the Government discontinuing the scheme, it was best to get out of this business. A couple of years later the scheme is now defunct and the Government have introduced a different type of tax saving for parents which they run through their own tax scheme.

This threat to one of my businesses prompted me to look carefully at setting up another business to replace it, which I still run.

By completing your own SWOT analysis, you will be able to get a better understanding of your business and be ready to tackle any issue that you might uncover. Moving on, you are now in a position to set some goals and follow up with action plans to counter some of the negative areas that you uncovered in your SWOT.

**Writing a business plan**

You want maximum success for your business, so you should think things through and plan for all eventualities. This is why we write a business plan. It will help you to:

• focus your business ideas
• identify potential problems
• set your aims and goals
• measure your progress

Business owners often write a business plan if they require funding to help them set up or grow their business. However, a well thought out business plan can become a highly effective tool, one which you can check regularly to see how you are getting on and adjust from time to time as your priorities change. You should view your business plan as a working document which is out on your desk more than it is in the drawer and is continually being tweaked.

By putting all your ideas for your business in one place it clarifies what it is that you are aiming for (the end); the plan then helps to get you to your ultimate goal.

A quick search of the internet will show you that there are many and varied business plan templates out there, some free, some not, for you to access. I have put together a simple business plan for you to use if you wish, cutting out everything that I think is unnecessary for the first-time business owner. As you get more confident, you can alter the original or abandon it and move onto a more complicated business plan template. As long as you are using it and it serves your purpose, it doesn't really matter what kind you use.

Let's start with the terminology of a standard business plan so that you understand what you should be writing within each section. When you have this knowledge, you will be able to decide how to present your own business plan.

**Simple Business Plan**

1. Business owner details -if you want to show this to someone else. How do they contact you?

2. Elevator pitch and strap or tag line – we've already been through your elevator pitch; your strap line is a very short sentence, two or three words that can sum up your business. Try to think a bit differently here, again to differentiate yourself from the competition and capture attention.

3. Executive summary – business summary and aims including a financial summary (profit and loss with costings.)

4. Owner's background - why you? This is like a mini CV linked to your present business/work/studies. For example, if you headed up a team at your last job, talk about that if it's relevant. You don't need to mention your Saturday job when you were 16, unless there is some special significance.

5. Products and services – what do you sell or provide? Be specific about this, now and in the future.

6. The market – who will buy, feasibility study? The work you did earlier will come in handy here, as you can show that you have thought about this being a feasible proposition.

7. How will you market the product? There is a chapter later in this book on marketing and branding which will help with this section. You will need to work out how you will find your customers and how they will find you, what your target market is and how you will get your products or services to them.

8. Competitors – who else is out there? You could put in a SWOT analysis here to show that you have thought of your business from every angle.

9. Operations and logistics. How will you organize your administration and the general running of your business? Will you need premises and equipment? If so, what and how much will these things cost?

10. Costs and pricing strategy – details about how much you will charge for each unit of your product, or each use of your service, etc. You will need to show that there is profit in this business, so think carefully about your pricing.

11. Financial forecasts and planning. When you know how much you are going to charge and how much you expect to sell over what period, you can make financial forecasts – working out how

much you can earn from your business over a certain period. Great fun. You may even go back and relook at your pricing strategy.

12. Contingency plans. This is something that cannot be ignored. You need to get all your contingencies in place. Try to think of every eventuality and plan for it. Hopefully, you will not need to use your contingencies.

> ***On your own:***
> Find a business plan that appeals to you and have a go at writing your first business plan.

**Ongoing plans**

If you are a planner, business will be a joy. You have just learned how to write a business plan which can be used to help you secure funding or just to have an overview of your business. You should also have plans which keep you focused every month, week and day. I recommend that you think about how you work best before you start your business and develop a storage system for your plans, then stick to it.

For example, I write down all sorts of things in A5 notebooks. I usually have at least one with me to jot down ideas and thoughts. I like them to look nice so choose ones with patterns or bright colours. I particularly like the ones without lines in them as I feel this gives me more scope to sketch out my ideas and to put things into boxes with arrows, etc. I put anything and everything down in the notebook and then transfer my ideas, as necessary, onto other planning sheets. I also write my goals in the notebooks.

It's a really useful and fulfilling exercise to go back through the notebooks and see how much you have achieved. It also acts like a bit of a diary in terms of what you were thinking about at the time. More recently I have started to add dates at the top of each page so when I look back in the future, I can see where I was up to and what I was thinking about. It's amazing how many times I see something written down in a notebook and then realise I have already achieved it a short while later. The notebooks are private and messy but make fantastic (personal) reading later. You can see how far you have come in your business journey and it gives you confidence demonstrating what you have achieved.

**Planning for your business every quarter**

One of the most useful plans I make in my business are 90 day plans or 'Quarterlies' as I like to call them, often shortened to 'Q Plan.'

**What is a Quarterly Plan?**

A Quarterly Plan sets out your goals for the next three months, 90 days or Quarter. If you divide the year into four you will need to do 4 Quarterlies per year. I like to fit in with traditional Quarters, so the new 90 day plans start on the 1st of January, April, July and October. There is an easy rhythm to this, and it means you start to plan for your next Quarter towards the end of the last. I put planning for each Quarter into my diary around the last week or so of December, March, June and September to organise my plans.

**How does it work?**

I always do my Quarterly plans on an Excel spreadsheet. You may find a quick search on the internet will come up with a proforma to use if you prefer. In essence, down the side of your spreadsheet you have a space for your goals, 3-7 is enough, many more and you will find the task unmanageable. I break each goal down into smaller areas, putting the calendar dates along the top for the next three months.

This example shows a simple Quarterly plan (Q Plan). I have only included one goal (which has four tasks to do). You can add up to 7 goals in your Excel spreadsheet and each will have some tasks to do, probably between 2 and 5 tasks per goal.

| Title of your plan | January | | | | | February | | | | March | | | |
|---|---|---|---|---|---|---|---|---|---|---|---|---|---|
| | 2 | 9 | 16 | 23 | 30 | 7 | 14 | 21 | 28 | 7 | 14 | 21 | 28 |
| $1^{st}$ Goal description: Couple of words | | | | | | | | | | | | | |
| 1. Break down into task | | | | | | | | | | | | | |
| 2. Break down into task | | | | | | | | | | | | | |
| 3. Break down into task | | | | | | | | | | | | | |
| 4. Break down into task | | | | | | | | | | | | | |

Once everything is in place, you should allocate a timescale for each goal or task. By putting each week separately along the top, you can see what needs doing at the start of the week and what it is that you may have to complete. Don't worry if it doesn't go to plan to start with, it is your own plan and you will get better.

> **TIP**
> If you use a traffic light system it makes it easy to see where you are up to in your plan; red means yet to start, orange means you have started working on it, green is completed.

The next example shows the Q Plan taking shape. You can see that the title in this example is about refurbishing a premises entrance and the first goal is to decorate the display boards, another goal may be to paint the walls, and another may be to buy new furniture. The goal is then broken down into manageable tasks. For each task, a date will be decided when to do this, depending on other tasks that need doing and your time commitments. The relevant box(es) will be shaded in. If for example, you had the meeting on $17^{th}$ January, you would shade in the box of the week beginning $16^{th}$ January. Obviously, you would put the tasks in the best order possible as some tasks need to be done first.

| Title: Office entrance refurbishment | January | | | | | February | | | | March | | | |
|---|---|---|---|---|---|---|---|---|---|---|---|---|---|
| $1^{st}$ Goal: Decorate display boards in entrance | 2 | 9 | 16 | 23 | 30 | 7 | 14 | 21 | 28 | 7 | 14 | 21 | 28 |
| | | | | | | | | | | | | | |
| Meeting to discuss colours and plan | | | (shaded) | | | | | | | | | | |
| Order materials | | | (shaded) | | | | | | | | | | |
| Stage One - put up all base material and paint | | | | (shaded) | | | | | | | | | |
| Stage Two – redo signage and put up | | | | | (shaded) | | | | | | | | |

One advantage of using this system is that you can see at a glance where you are up to if you keep it up to date, particularly if you use colours rather than grey scale, as in the example. In my businesses we always have Q Plans and all managers are taught how to use them. We keep them online so they can be shared easily. This can be highly motivational for staff who have completed Q Plans, as their line manager can see where they are up to and comment on their progress.

One disadvantage (or advantage depending on how you view it) of using the Q Plan system is that you really have to think when setting it up until you get used to doing it. I use my notes gathered over time to decide my priorities. One thing to look out for is thinking you should (or could) do everything on the Q Plan in the first week, or at least starting it all at the same time, especially if you are really enthusiastic about each goal.

To counter this, it may be useful to ask someone else to look over your Q Plan when you have finished writing it. You will see for yourself that if you have a lot of red squares, all starting at the beginning of the plan, you will need to spread them out a bit. In addition, you should look at what is happening in your life and in your business. If you have a family holiday booked for week three, there's no point in booking appointments with people or setting certain tasks. However, this may be an opportunity to catch up on any relevant reading or research that you may need to do.

**Action plans**

From your Q Plan you are now ready to look at breaking down the areas into action plans. An action plan is just that – it is a plan of action. You will find examples of action plans on the internet for you to adapt or use, depending on how you like to work. They are all largely the same in content, but you may prefer a certain layout depending on how you like to work. Spend some time deciding on which type of action plan you like, then stick to it until you find a better one, as you can save your action plan as a template to re-use.

Action plans have:
• A set goal or aim – usually just one simple statement at a time.
• Smaller, more achievable tasks underneath this, starting to break down the goal into specific actions.
• A person responsible – this is for accountability. When you are starting out, this is probably mainly going to be you.
• A time frame – how long this is expected to take and when this will happen. It is very important that it is time-bound, as this creates a sense of urgency and momentum to your task.
• Resources required - is sometimes on action plans. This is always on mine as sometimes this involves funding an action or, more often, someone's time, which is also a resource.

You can either handwrite your action plans or type them, print them out to put up on your walls or keep them in a handy online place. The main thing is that you use them. There's no point in making these plans for them to go into a drawer or online file never to be seen again.

Action plans offer a sense of purpose and should be easy to follow, giving you confidence when you have completed them, as each small action goes towards making the larger action or goal possible. They keep you in check and are very useful to help clarify your focus when you are writing them. I find it is better for the person who will be doing them to write them. Receiving a version of someone else's action plan without explanation can be difficult.

You will need to set aside some time for writing your plans, but it will be worth it. Immersing yourself in your business in this way can clarify where you are going, then it is just a simple step-by-step approach as to how to get there.

**Goal setting / SMART action plans**

**Goals are different from actions**

When you set goals for yourself and your business you should also set a time limit for those goals. Goals are long term aims. For example, you may want to be able to give up your day job by this time next year. Breaking down this goal requires a little extra thought. Let's say you currently earn £30,000 per year and work for 35 hours per week, with a holiday entitlement of 30 days. Firstly, we need to work out which language to use.

**Mind your language**

A goal for the above may be written as:

> *By January, I will be working 30 hours per week in my own business. The business will consistently bring in a minimum of £3000 per month, even when I am on holiday.*

A couple of things I did there. Firstly, I gave you a pay rise to £36,000 per year, then I reduced your hours. Secondly, the goal was written as if it is going to be achieved. Positive thinking and speaking can go a long way towards getting what you want. The more specific your goals and aims, the better, as it gives your brain something concrete to work with. Lastly, the goal was written down. I am not sure how this one works but I can honestly say that after 20 years in business, somehow something magical happens when you write things down. I presume that it's your brain focusing on the task and looking for opportunities on your behalf that all adds up to taking you towards your goals.

**Sizeable chunks**

Next comes the part where you break this goal down into smaller, more manageable and achievable pieces or chunks. For the above example, start at the end and work backwards - starting with the end in mind - sound familiar?

The example gives you a couple of years to reach your goal. The components of this are to establish your new business and to give up your day job. Your action plans might comprise:

- training and additional knowledge needs
- setting up your new business structures
- starting your new business part-time to see if it works
- reducing your work hours to put more hours into your business

• saving some money to sustain yourself and your business
• seeking out funding to get you started
• getting all your business plans in place
• setting up marketing, advertising and social media presence for your new business.

You may have to write an action plan for each of the above to help you reach your goal. As you can see, it's a lot of work. You might think you can skip some of the stages, and you probably can, but remember you are trying to set up your business to give up your day job, so this needs to be right. All the above actions will need to be time-bound and sequenced. For example, you may decide to gain more knowledge or attend some training to help you to work in your business. That will obviously need to come before you start the business part-time and so on.

I have included a copy of the plan that I tend to use in my business as an example.

It is a **SMART** action plan.
**SMART** stands for:
**Specific** - being specific will help you to clarify exactly what you want
**Measurable** - measurable aims so that you know when you have achieved them
**Achievable** - there is no point setting yourself such a difficult task that it is unachievable
**Realistic** - make sure that you are being realistic, or you set yourself up to fail
**Timebound** - be specific about how long you expect each area to take or by when

Notes in each section give you an idea of what to put in each:

## Planning sheet for Business Growth Goals

| | | | | |
|---|---|---|---|---|
| **People** | Who will be involved? Who is this for? | | | |
| **Time Frame** | Could be January or a set of dates | **Responsible?** | Who will lead this action plan? | |
| **No.** | **Action Area** | **Task to do** | **By who, when?** | **Done** |
| 1 | Title of action goes here | I usually list a job or task specifically to do with the action area here | Write their initials and by when or a specific date | Tick or initial when task is done |
| 2 | These action areas are often to do with the same thing | | | |
| 3 | | | | |
| 4 | | | | |
| 5 | Five action areas is ample | The five areas may come from the breakdown of your goals on the Qplan | | |
| **Resources required, including meetings, etc.** | | **Other key people involved – at what stage?** | | |
| You may have to get things ready, so a brief list is good | | So that you can think about who to involve and then ask them to a meeting or to prepare something for you | | |
| **Notes:** This space is for anything that you may think of. I always like to have a space for my notes on any action plan. | | | | |

### Working IN and working ON your business

These are two distinct areas of working with your business and many people concentrate on only one of them, to the detriment of the other.

### Working IN your business

When you are working *in* your business you are doing the tasks and jobs that need doing. For example, if you run a flower shop, you may be working in your business from 9-5 when the shop is open, serving customers. You will also need to organize and take deliveries, make sure receipts and payments are up to date, and keep customers and staff happy. Working *in* your business consists of all the day-to-day running of your business.

**Working ON your business**

This is the other side of business, the one that often gets neglected, because of the time spent working *in* the business. When you are working *on* your business, you may be:

- networking with other business owners to bring in new customers
- putting together a business plan ready for some additional funding
- advertising and marketing the business through social media
- spending time with a mentor who is helping you to develop either yourself or your business systems

The time you allocate to working on and in your business is not equally divided. Sometimes they can run alongside each other. For example, in the flower shop, if there are no customers, you may spend 15 minutes updating your business plan. It is, however, important to give due regard to both working in and on your business. You can probably see how it would be easy to concentrate on working *in* your business and neglect working *on* the business. It is important to step outside of your routine and take a look at your business from the outside to see where you are going, what message you're putting out there and generally just to see your next move. When working on your business you are usually moving it forward in some way; working in your business is more static from a business point of view.

You may feel that working on your business is not a good use of time, particularly when you are really busy trying to run your company. However, you need to make time for both. If you just concentrate on one area you may find that either you have a business which, although busy, is not organized and is a bit stagnant, or if you go the other way, you may find you have lots of great plans in place but no real business to work them in. It's a careful balancing act.

**Chapter Takeaways**

This chapter concentrated on planning your new venture. Once you have decided which kind of business structure you are going to adopt, certain things have to be put in place. For example, if you want funding to start up your business, you will need to put a business plan in place, which is also useful as a guiding 'map' to your plans for development and growth. You learned how to do a SWOT sheet to analyse your business strengths, weaknesses, opportunities and threats.

Whether or not you want to put a business plan in place, you do need some sort of plan. I encourage you to write regular plans, from Qplans covering the next 90 days, down to action plans which keep your structure tight and help you achieve smaller steps, all going towards the success of your new business. You now understand the importance of and can have a go at, setting achievable (SMART) goals. Finally, we talked about the difference between working in and on your business and why you need to do both in order to move your business forward.

**Call to action**

Make a decision about your new business structure
Work out what you want a business to do for you
Begin with the end in mind
Clarity when writing a business plan
The importance of planning:

- Qplans
- Ongoing plans
- Smart action plans
- Breaking goals down into sizeable chunks
- Working IN and ON your business

*If you look after the pennies, the pounds will look after themselves.*

*Traditional Proverb*

# Chapter Three: Numbers

Know your business numbers. This is not just how much you have in the bank but also how much you are selling your goods and services for, whether you are making a profit and if so, by how much. I would advise that you start a routine that allows you to understand your numbers on a regular basis. By checking your bank accounts on a weekly or even daily basis you are in a good position to see what is happening, particularly if something doesn't look right or if you are close to your credit limit. With internet banking it is quick and easy to keep a constant check on what is happening. In my experience it also follows that when you know your numbers you are more in control of the financial aspect of your business.

> **TIP**
> Be annoyingly on the numbers.

**Your break-even point**

It is important to know your break-even point; you have perhaps heard others talk about this but may not be sure what it is? Your break-even is the point at which you have paid for everything and you are from then on making a profit. This is an important number to have a handle on because it is highly motivating and also ensures you keep a tight rein on your outgoings so you begin to make a profit as soon as possible.

Let's work through an example so you can see how it works.

**Example break-even point**
You have a hairdressing business in which you hire a chair in a salon. You specialise in colouring hair which pays well and has repeat business.
Your costs are as follows:
Chair in salon is £100 per week
Insurance is £5.25 per week
Resources e.g hair dyes, sprays, shampoo £25.00
Other – coffee, tea, etc. £4.25 per week
Total is £135.00 per week

If most customers average visit to the hairdresser is about £35.00 per time, then 4 customers (£35.00 x 4 = £140.00) are needed to break even. The actual breakeven point is £135.00 per week in this example so after 4 customers this business is making a profit.

If this hairdresser takes in 10 customers a week then turnover is about £350.00, take away the costs above = £135.00 so the profit available is £215.00 per week. You do need to pay tax on profit in your business, so HMRC would take some of this money. You may need to put money aside for your tax and National Insurance (NI) payments. If you are a basic taxpayer this would be about 20-25%. .... the rest is yours!
On the above example you may decide you could fit in 20 customers per week.
So £35 x 20 = £700 less costs = £700-£135 = £565
£565 x 25% = £141.25 saved for tax and NI
Total to you is £423.75

Another way to work out your breakeven point is how much each customer 'costs' you.
Using the above example, leaving out your tax and national insurance payments:
If you have ten customers paying £35.00 each customer is worth £21.50 to you.
If you have twenty customers they are worth £28.25 each to you.
It's worth playing with the numbers now that you understand the principle.

As you can see, you can work out all sorts of figures and scenarios based on your break-even point and it's important to know all your incoming and outgoing costs so you can play with the numbers. *The tax and national insurance may not be as above as we all currently get a personal allowance which is tax free, but I think you can see what I am trying to explain.

**The cost of set up and running your business**

Other costs that you need to consider when you are setting up your new business are the initial or start-up costs. As I don't know your individual business and what you intend to do it will be quite difficult for me to be specific in this section. However, I can give you some ideas as to the type of costs that most businesses will encounter and need to plan for.

If you set up a limited company (or partnership) there will be initial costs for the set up. Some companies, solicitors and accountants offer a service to set up a limited company for a fee, but it is not a complicated process so you should shop around for a simple and cost effective set up price. If you are going to set up as a sole trader to start with, there are no real costs involved in establishing the company as an entity.

Premises may or may not be a consideration for you in terms of set up costs. If you need specific premises, you may have to consider a lease. Apart from the actual rent payable, you will need to engage a solicitor, as this is a legal document and you will need to be sure about what you are signing. A quick internet search will help you to find a solicitor who is used to dealing with commercial leases locally, or you could ask the letting agent for a recommendation. If you are in a position to buy your premises then you will need to think about costs for a surveyor and solicitor, bank loan costs or a commercial mortgage.

**Rent and rates**

We once had a business many years ago for which we required premises straight away. We found the ideal place in the centre of our town. The building required some cosmetic enhancement, so we painted, cleaned and generally spruced up the place before we opened for business.

However, we had two main problems with the site, both of which in hindsight made the premises unsuitable for us. Firstly, we hadn't realised that the rates payable for a town centre site would be so much. The rates per month were far in excess of the rent, rendering our original break-even figures out of synch.

Secondly, we operated from the upstairs of a building. The ground floor was rented to a couple who restored furniture. Upstairs had been empty for some time before we took over and as a result, the ground floor occupants had been using our allocated parking. One of the reasons we liked the site was for the parking spaces as our customers were coming and going all the time. The people downstairs made our life very difficult for wanting to use our own parking spaces, often blocking us and our customers in as an intimidation tactic.

The moral of the tale is two-fold and you can learn from our mistakes. We should have sought better clarity on both the rates and the parking situation before we signed the lease. The furniture people soon went out of business (possibly due to them not being very nice people?) and we moved our premises to one with cheaper rates a bit further out of town with no parking issues

**What about working from home?**
Increasingly, and more recently due to the worldwide pandemic, many people are setting up their businesses from home. This is a great low-cost and convenient idea. However, it does have its drawbacks:

1. You have to be very self-disciplined to work from home so as not to get distracted by day-to-day things happening around you.
2. You will probably need some allocated space for your 'work' stuff.

3. Confidentiality may be an issue depending on the type of business you operate.
4. You may require help (from a paid accountant) to sort out what you can claim for as business expenses in the home and this in turn may affect your mortgage or your council tax.
5. It's quite lonely working by yourself at home all day without the interaction of others, particularly if you have been used to a busy work environment.
6. It can sometimes show or be perceived as a lack of professionalism, depending on your business type.
7. You may find having your office at home means you never switch off, because you can always find something to do, or other people think that you are always 'open'.
8. Other people may not fully understand you are working, therefore are not available (as would be the case if you were out at work somewhere).

**Home office**

In 2004 we were very excited when we moved to a larger house which had an office downstairs. This meant we could operate our business from our house, less travel time and costs, available at home most of the time, etc. The reality was quite different.

We were running our childcare business at the time and parents would book by emailing or completing and sending a booking form for their children to attend one of our Out of School Clubs, based in many schools in 5 different local authorities.

Customers would often come to the house at any time of the day or late evening, putting a lot of pressure on the family. We were being forced to work constantly due to people telephoning and calling in at the house. It was also difficult to relax at home. We recognised that our business was not suitable for a home environment, so began the search for an independent office

**Business stationery**

You will need to decide whether you need business stationery or not. This can be anything from business cards to letter headed paper, to compliment slips. When we used to send items by post, we found we needed letterheaded paper and compliment slips. More recently we have moved most of our business online, so find that compliment slips are rarely required. Letterheaded paper is still requested when you are setting up accounts with firms, or if you need to send out certain letters, e.g. debt letters or reference letters. Business cards can be a useful marketing tool. When you meet new people in business, they often swap business cards.

With all your business stationery there will be printing costs and in some cases design costs as well. If you are having a logo this will incur a one-off cost and is well worth the investment. You can find local designers and printers online and they often have deals for you to tap into. A word of warning though, some logo designers and business card printers are very cheap for the initial run of stationery. However, after the first print run, the price tends to go up to a normal price – so watch out for that. Also watch out for copyright. In some cases, your logo will belong to someone else. Make sure you are clear about whose logo it is.

**What about equipment?**

What sort of equipment do you need and how much will it cost? Are you able to use your personal computer? Is it capable of carrying out the tasks you need it to? Or do you want to have a laptop or desktop which is solely dedicated to your new project? Will you need a printer? How much is ink? Furniture required may be as simple as a desk and chair, which you may already have. Or do you need specialist equipment to operate your business? Do you have to buy, or can it be leased or rented?

Sometimes it's cheaper to lease equipment so you can have it upgraded frequently and have peace of mind that it is going to work for you every time. What about the internet? Do you have it where you are setting up your business or is this a new expense? And your phone; are you going to use your personal mobile for the business? Do you have a land line (that you could

also divert to a mobile)? How about normal stationery? Do you need paper, pens, general office equipment?
Of course, you will already have much of the above but is it the right thing to use them? Is it better to have work and personal separate and what is the estimated cost of doing this?
You may decide to start off using your own equipment, then in time buy items for your business through your business.

**Employees?**

In one of my first businesses I had to have someone in place on the first day of opening, so I have almost always had people working for and with me. This is an expense in itself, which we go into in more detail in Chapter Seven. For now, you need to think about how you advertise for staff, if required, which may involve some sort of budget.

**Where does all this money come from to set up?**

By now you may feel a bit overwhelmed by the costs that you (could) incur so far. From premises to insurance (make sure you have the correct type for your business class in place before you start), to equipment and stationery. It all costs money and you will need to work out a) what you need to set up your business and b) where you are going to get everything from, i.e. rent or buy, borrow or make do. If you are buying lots of new things for your business, be sure to know that you need them, that you can afford them and where the money is coming from to acquire them, plus you will need to keep all receipts. You should also make comprehensive lists of things that you have for your business to make it work in the form of an inventory, which you can update as your business grows. We cover more about paperwork in Chapter Five.

**Your expected ongoing costs**

After the set-up costs, you should consider the day-to-day running costs of your business, which we call ongoing costs. These will be due on a regular basis, some of which will be a regular amount, others different amounts each month.

You may need to pay:

1. an accountant or bookkeeper depending on what type of company structure you have
2. staff wages, if applicable
3. pension and PAYE costs
4. accountant or payroll company to process your wages
5. a bank reconciliation program, like Xero or QuickBooks
6. bank fees
7. loan repayments
8. broadband and anti-virus fees
9. website hosting fees
10. stationery and consumables
11. marketing budget
12. compliance – regulatory bodies, insurance costs
13. rent and rates
14. renewing or leasing equipment
15. utility bills, like gas, water, electricity
16. subscription payments e.g. Dropbox account or similar

And so on. Some of the above will be relevant to you and you may need to make additions for your own particular business.

The above is not an exhaustive list and is not written to scare you. It's true, there are lots of ongoing payments to think about, but my view is that if you have thought of everything before-hand there is less likely to be a shock when your business gets going. You will also be able to work out your break-even point more easily as you will be better informed.

You will have to make an educated guess as to how much any of the above is going to cost you initially and whether you need all of the items. If, for example, you don't need to employ anyone else in your business that negates several of the above costs.

Once you have an idea of what your ongoing costs might be, you will be able to set targets for your income.

**Income Targets Example**

Let's say you would like to earn a £24000 profit per year from a coaching business. Firstly, we need to guestimate the tax and NI costs. If half of the income required is approximately your personal allowance, you will pay tax on the other half. Your estimated tax will be 25%, so to achieve £24000 you will probably need an income of around £27000.

Next let's look at your ongoing costs, which you have worked out to be £1500 per month including a start-up loan repayment. Your running or ongoing costs will be about £18000 per year. Add this to your income requirements and you will see how much you need to bring in each year. £27000 plus £18000 = £45000.

We'll add a bit of contingency onto that (and to make the figures really easy!) - £3000 per year. Total required in this simple model is £48000 per year or £4000 per month. If you take on coaching clients who pay on average £2000 each, you will need 2 per month to cover your costs. If you know that customers dry up in December, you will need to take three new clients on for two of the other months to make sure you hit your targets.

With these smaller figures the tax you pay is around about the same whether it is through corporation tax and dividends on your profit (limited company), or if it's just you as a sole trader to start.

**Setting up a bank account**

If you are serious about your business, you will need a separate business bank account. I say if you are serious because if you start as you mean to go on, your accounting and reconciliation will be straightforward. Some people mistakenly think it's ok to use their personal bank account and sort it out later. In my view that is very dangerous, as the business money might be used for personal expenses and everything gets into a muddle. It's not difficult to open a bank account, particularly if you have a personal one already (as some checks are already available on you).

The two main concerns for the banks are money laundering and whether you need a loan.

Banks have checks imposed on them to ensure clients are bona-fide; this is the reason why you are asked questions about your business. Although I prefer to do things face-to-face, this option became more difficult during the Covid-19 pandemic, however, you can open a business bank account online, particularly if you are a UK resident with other bank accounts and ID (like your driving licence) online in the UK system.

When deciding which bank to choose there are a few things to consider, such as; ability to withdraw your money and make payments; whether you need an overdraft or a loan from the bank; where your start-up money is coming from; what kind of banking you expect to do; and whether the bank you choose offers you support from a bank manager. This can be a great help to a start-up business, as your bank manager deals with all manner of businesses on a daily basis, so is in a good position to give advice and help.

By doing a simple internet search you can find out all these things and I suggest you compare them, so you choose the best one for your situation. For example, if you are only dealing with online payments by BACs, an online only tariff from the banks is usually cheaper. If you need to deposit cheques, look at the charges for this, as you will have to offset this against your banking fees and in turn, the prices charged to customers. Similarly, if you want to accept card payments over the phone or online you will need a bank account that can do this, which comes with additional charges. You may want to collect payments via a card reader out and about, again you will need a bank account to pay these directly into. If you think you need an overdraft, look at the charges and when they apply.

Also, look at fee free periods which most business banks will offer for the beginning of your time with them, ranging from 12 to 24 months.

> **TIP**
> As soon as your bank account is open you will start on your fee free tariff, even if you don't have any money in the bank or are not using the account. You should therefore be mindful as to when you open the account, so you can take the most benefit from your fee free period.

You may need a business plan (see Chapter Two) if you want to borrow money from the bank. The bank will be interested in what risk *you* are taking with this venture. What that means in practice is how much money are you putting into the project. By adding in your own funds, the bank can see you are serious about your business; that reduces the risk for them. If you need a substantial amount of money, you may be asked to hand over the deeds to your house, if you have one. The bank will not happily lend you money to pay yourself a wage, you are expected to earn that. However, if you need money to buy equipment or against a deposit for a lease on the premises, they may be more willing.

**Other money sources**

The banks are not the only institutions lending money. If you need funds to set up your business, consider the following:

- You and your savings
- Personal credit cards and overdrafts
- Re-mortgaging your assets
- Your family and friends
- Joint venturing with someone else or a sponsor
- An investor
- Peer to peer lending

The first three are about you 'lending' yourself the money to start your business. The advantages of this are that you will not owe anything to anyone, and the business would be totally owned by you. Obvious disadvantages are that you could get yourself into personal debt or financial difficulty trying to finance the set-up of your new business. If this is the case, why would anyone else lend you money, including the banks? If you have confidence in your product or service and your ability to start the business and make a success of it, this shouldn't be as much of a risk. This is why the book began with looking at your suitability as a business owner and the suitability of your business in the market. It also links with you keeping your 'day job' until you are in a good position to move into your new business full time. It's about risk management. Being an entrepreneur is often seen as risky, but most entrepreneurs will not take unnecessary risks.

**Risk Perception**

Most people assume that entrepreneurs are big risk takers and a bit 'gung-ho' in their attitude to risk. However, a study by Simon, Houghton and Aquino (Cognitive biases, risk perception, and venture formation: How individuals decide to start companies, 2000) highlighted that it is risk perception rather than actual risk which separates entrepreneurs from non-entrepreneurs. This is based on three keys:

- Over-confidence in themselves and their products and services (remember the Something To Think About in chapter one on over-optimism?)
- An illusion of control; this is where the entrepreneur believes they have more control over a situation than they actually have
- Relying on small samples for information, particularly if the small sample presents a favourable outcome for the entrepreneur.

In practice what this can mean for the entrepreneur is that they misjudge the risk involved in a situation. Due to risk perception, an entrepreneur may not move forward with an idea and the risk therefore becomes a barrier to success. This can also play a part in whether to actually start and set up your business. If the perceived risk is too high, you should not go ahead.

I think you need to weigh up the pros and cons of a business opportunity before rushing in, which is partly why we are going steadily through this book. If you think there is a risk (perceived), check it out against the three keys above.

- Are you being a bit overconfident or over-optimistic?
- Do you have control of the situation or are there things outside your control which will, or could, adversely affect you or your business?
- Where did you get your information from? How extensive and reliable was your research?

By answering the questions above as honestly as you can, you will lessen your exposure to risk. Entrepreneurs are not the biggest risk takers. By calculating and considering carefully, no-one can say that you have a gung-ho attitude, or take unnecessary risks.

The last four in the list relate to gaining funding from elsewhere. A word of caution – all on this list will want to know what you have put into the business yourself, due to them taking a risk with their own funds. If you are asking other people or institutions to lend you money, they will want something back which may be in the form of part of your business. Think very carefully about this. Do you want to give away some or any of your business to someone else? They will naturally want to know what's in it for them. You need to be sure you can make repayments on time and how this will fit in with your plans. For example, a family member might say, pay me when you can. However, an investor may want a stake in your business, and a percentage of profit. You would need to consider whether you want someone to have this kind of hold over you and your business. Other lenders will want to know that you have a viable business before risking lending money, so it may be tricky to access funding from peer-to-peer platforms until your business is more established, perhaps when you have built it up a little whilst still working in your day job.

**Money in - where from?**
When choosing your bank account, you should consider where your money is coming from. How will your customers and clients pay you? At this very early stage of your business it is up to you how you get paid. I suggest you think carefully about this so it can be established now for the long term. You can add the payments criteria to your terms and conditions, your bank details for payment to invoices and so on. We cover what kind of paperwork you need for your business in Chapter Five.

I would advise against taking cash payments into your business if possible. This is because cash is less traceable, and you are more likely to confuse which is your personal money and what belongs to the business. If you have cash on-site, you are also putting yourself and your business in a potentially dangerous position. If you are known not to take cash, there may be less chance of you being targeted for theft. Plus, by sending everything through the bank account you have an online check for every transaction you make which enables you to re-assess your break-even point along the way or when introducing new products and services. It also gives you peace of mind that you are not going to get into trouble with your tax. In addition, if in the future you want to borrow some money or extend your business, your bank account will show everything you need to know about what goes in and what comes out which takes all the guesswork out of how your business runs.

You may need a little bit of cash for incidentals, e.g. if you run out of milk at the office or need some stamps. This is what we call petty cash. I operate this in the very same way, by writing everything down that has been paid for with cash into a small book. For example, you draw out £20.00 from your business bank account for petty cash. In your book you write £20.00 at the top of the page. You buy some milk at £1.50. You write 'milk £1.50' in your book and make a new total of £18.50. You pop the receipt for the milk into your book or a small folder to prove that you bought it. The money you have left in your petty cash book is £18.50 and should always be exact. Literally, take the cash out with you and put the change back in the petty cash pot.

Some people find dealing with cash difficult and worrisome but if you stick to a few simple rules and always follow them, you'll be fine.

**Systems to help you reconcile your bank accounts**

I suggest that you reconcile your bank accounts regularly, either by keeping a spread sheet yourself so you know where all your money is coming from, or by using a reconciliation system like Xero or Quickbooks. Both operate in a similar way in that they pull your transactions directly from your bank for you, then you assign them to specific areas. For example, if you have a regular payment from a client, you could reconcile that to 'Sales' (money in), if you need to pay your rent once a month this will be reconciled to 'Rent' and so on. With both systems you can send out invoices. When the system begins to recognise regular payments in or out it will suggest this to you, making reconciliation quick and easy. There is a charge associated with using these systems and others like it, so you may want to investigate whether using one is going to be beneficial to you, particularly if you only have a few customers and bills to pay.

You are also in control of when people pay you. You can ask for immediate payment, payment up front or on invoice, giving, for example, 30 days for someone to pay. You can ask for payments to be made on a certain date, perhaps because you know that you have your own bills to be paid soon after. In one of my businesses we request that payment is made on the 1$^{st}$ of each month. This is because payments are due out by the 5$^{th}$ of each month from the same account. In addition, it means that I only have to check the bank account once in this business, which is very time efficient. It also means I am quick to notice if anyone hasn't paid and can send a reminder requesting payment.

**Loans for your business**

We have already touched on where you can borrow money from beyond your own savings, but how do you go about getting a loan from a bank or lending company?

Firstly, you will need to have a business plan. If you are planning on asking for money to start your business, your business plan will need to be detailed and clear. What lenders are looking for is feasibility, structure and profit. Some lenders have their own template for you to complete.

**Feasibility**

Is this a good idea? What need is there for this kind of business? You will need to quantify. For example, if you want to run an organic food delivery service, you will need to quantify the need for such a service in your area. You may have to do surveys to ask people if they would be interested in your product, whether they would use such a service, if organic fresh food is important to them, etc. Next you would need to look at the competition. Who else is out there doing something similar? If there is no-one in your area, where and who is the nearest competition. It's great to be the first to do something but is there a reason why others have not tried this in your area? Do they know something about your intended customer base or other local competition? It could be that the local supermarket has an extensive organic range using local farmers and an established delivery service, so there may be no need for your service. Lenders will want to see that you have thought about this and have numbers to back it up.

Earlier we talked about risk; lending money to a new business is very risky. The more information you can give the better. If there are 10,000 people within a 3-mile radius, 10% of whom are vegan and prefer organic foods, you could potentially reach out to 1000 people with your service. Not all would be interested, however it may be a good start. Where do you find these people? Is there a neighbourhood group that you could join to canvass opinion? The more thorough you can be in your feasibility study the better. It will give you confidence in your intended market and more importantly, any lender will have confidence that there is a market out there waiting for your service. If you are one of many out there, how is your product or service different? What is your USP and what makes you worth backing financially?

**Structure**

This is where structure comes in. Throughout this book and coming up in the next few chapters, you will learn about how to structure your business, which is important to those looking at lending money to you. They need to have confidence in the business owner (you!), and in the team, if applicable. The confidence will come from prior experience in the business field, for example, if you wish to start a business teaching people how to arrange flowers, if you are currently a florist with 6 years' experience then you probably have the credentials to teach others flower arranging. If your experience lies in marketing and you have two team members who are expert flower arrangers. Again, this will give confidence to any potential lender.

The way you present your business will be important too. If you can show you have all the business structures in place, that you have thought about how to run the business, you will instil confidence in a would-be lender. When looking at who to lend money to, lenders look at the person behind the business, the driving force, the one that will keep it going. You will be judged on many things, after all, the ball is very firmly in their court. Yes, you will pay the interest on any loan, yes, you may have to risk your own home to get a loan, but at the end of the day, if the lender does not have confidence in you and your ability to run the business effectively, however good the idea, they are not lending to you. So, don't tip up to a meeting after rolling out of bed with a few scraps of paper in your hand showing some ideas. Make the effort to show that this is important to you by making anything you take along to support your application (including yourself) - look professional. Give potential lenders confidence that you have a professional, well thought out structure in place to start your business. It will give *you* confidence too and that will show.

**Profit**

Of course, a potential lender, particularly if it is an investor, will want to see that your business idea will make a profit. A good business makes money. A profitable business goes beyond the break-even (see earlier in the chapter). With a new business you are not expected to make a profit on day one. Some of you might (hurray!), but most will take a little longer. The important thing when asking for money from someone else is to be realistic about when and how much money you are going to make. If you don't know your numbers or they are unrealistic, you will fail in your attempt to secure funding. A spreadsheet is useful to show exactly when you expect to be making a profit. You can use formulas to work things out for you and most people are familiar with the layout so can understand them. If spreadsheets are unfamiliar to you, then I suggest you take a short course, as being comfortable with spreadsheets will save you a lot of time.

Be prepared for lenders to test you on your spreadsheet and have the answers ready. For example, in your new widget company, you may be asked why you are only charging 20p per widget when you could make more profit by charging 30p. Your answer may be along the lines of, 'Having looked at competitors, I feel confident that at 20p we are in line with the normal charging band. Our widgets are not larger than others and although we could charge 30p each, we would exclude too much of the market. At 20p we remain competitive in a very competitive market without being too cheap or expensive.' The lender feels confident that you have explored the options of price increase and have a good answer as to why the price should be set at 20p for now. You have shown that although at a higher price you could make a more substantial profit, you recognise that at that level you may not sell much stock.

**Responsibility**

When you take out a loan you take on a huge responsibility. You have to repay it with interest over a set period of time. This is the case even when your business is not doing well or has a bad month. For this reason, you will need to budget carefully and consider your other expenses before taking out the loan. If, for example, your business is quiet in the summer months, you will need to make sure you have enough saved to make essential payments; your loan repayment is one of those. The loan could also be linked to a personal asset, making timely repayments even more important.

Think carefully about how much you need to ask for and don't get any more. It's tempting to ask for more than you require so that you have a 'slush fund' but this is a dangerous move. Firstly, you will have to prove why you want more (and to pay yourself more is not a good reason!). Secondly, you have to pay back more with interest so again, not really a smart move.

**The importance of recording transactions**

So, who is interested in what money you make and how you make it?

Well YOU for a start. This is your new business. You will need to know for sure – no guessing or estimating – exactly what you are earning from your new business and how much you are spending on it. The banks need to know that you are making money a) in case you have a loan to repay and b) in case you are in danger of going overdrawn. Your accountant or bookkeeper will be interested in what you are earning so that your tax payable can be worked out and of course HMRC will want to know what you are taking in, less expenses, so that you can be charged the correct personal or company tax on your profit, depending on your business structure.

It is important to keep all your numbers, income and outgoings, receipts and expenses in good and accessible order. This information can be kept on spreadsheets or you can use a commercial system, as discussed previously. Apart from people outside your business wanting to know you are doing well, you need to know this yourself. You will not be able to plan for your new business unless you know how much 'spare' money there is after everything has been paid.

Say, for example, you want to buy some new machinery. You would obviously need to know the cost and the benefit having this piece of machinery would bring to your business. If the machine costs £1000.00 and is expected to last 5 years, the machine costs you an average of £200.00 per year. If by having the new machine you can increase production, bringing in on average an extra £800.00 per year, the machine would be worth the investment. A simple example but you get the idea. If your business cannot afford £1000.00 for a machine at the moment, you will need to look at other ways of finding the money. A loan at 8% would eat into your profit but not by as much as the machine would benefit your business. Or what about leasing the machine? If on our simple figures, the machine was £100.00 per year to rent, this may be a safer option. By knowing your numbers, you will be in a position to make decisions like these all the time and work out the benefits of moving your business forward.

Knowing your numbers helps you to set income and expenditure (outgoings) targets. If you know your break-even point you can work out how much income you are targeting. Whichever way you record your numbers, keep it in a safe place (online?) and keep it updated, making it easier to work things out at the end of the year when you need to show how your business has been doing over the past twelve months. This would also be a good time to check in and update your business plan if you have one, so that you are very much up to date.

Start as you mean to go on with your financial transactions. Don't do anything unnecessary but work out how you like to see things written down – it could be a coloured spreadsheet or a bespoke programme or free sheet from the internet, then try to stick with it so that there is continuity across your business. It is also quicker when you are completing spreadsheets because you are familiar with the layout.

**Don't give up your day job**

For most people, starting your own business is a risk. You may well have a job to give up. For some, entrepreneurship or running your own business, may have been a long-term aim but life has got in the way with bills to pay and so on. When you were at school possibly no-one mentioned that you could work for yourself, make your own way in the world and make your own money.

When setting up your own business it is a huge leap for this reason; very few will completely give up their day job or any financial security they have when starting up, to avoid the risk of a financial meltdown. Most people start small, taking 'baby steps' towards their dream of owning their own business and being financially free from their day job. For some this happens quickly, for others less so. The security of keeping a regular income from employed work, is too cosy to give up entirely, and that's okay; it's fine to be cautious. As we said earlier, entrepreneurs are known to be risk takers, but successful entrepreneurs calculate the risk involved and start from there.

As an example, let's assume you have income from somewhere when you start to think about your new venture. In order to make the shift from employee to business owner, you may have to become a part time business owner before you release yourself from your employed income and become a self-sufficient entrepreneur. What you need to think about here is not just money but also the currency of time. Everyone has a set amount of time in their day; how you choose to use that time could make a difference to when you finish work and concentrate fully on your new business. If you start your business on a smaller scale, if this is possible, you will be able to do both 'jobs' at the same time. The reason I talk about the currency of time is that you may have to reduce your leisure time to run two things at once. In addition, from your business point of view, you can look for opportunities to enhance your business whilst still in your day job. For example, on your commute to work listen to podcasts, Clubhouse or training courses that will help you in your business. Consider your friendship groups to enable you to be amongst the people that you need to be working and mixing with for your business. If you are focussed, it becomes easier to do. By focussing on your business and writing out your goals and plans, you will automatically make choices to benefit it.

In the last chapter we looked at goal setting and planning for your business; now you can put those plans in place to help you achieve at the early stage of taking on your own business. Don't worry that the pace is slowed by keeping your day job; you are keeping your security, which there's a lot to be said for. You don't want to add to your worries or be seen as reckless by others, particularly those who you may want financial support from. In addition, your job can provide you with invaluable skills and experiences which may help you in your business. There are many skills we take for granted in our working life, such as customer service skills, telephone manner, etc. All these basic skills, which we acquire subconsciously, will prove invaluable when you come to work for yourself and set your own rules, even if you think the company you work for doesn't get it right. In your own business you have the opportunity to take what you have learned, good and bad and change it to fit your business.

One area you do need to be mindful of is taking business away from your employer. You may be setting up a consultancy to offer a very similar service. If you are, you will need to think carefully about the customers you already have through your work. Your contract may stipulate that you are unable to access any of your 'work' customers for a period of time once you have left. This is to protect the employment of your colleagues left behind as much as anything. Also, from an ethical viewpoint, if you did go behind your employers back to access their customers, how would you feel, having potentially breached your contract? It also doesn't make for good reading on a business plan that you are getting your customers from someone else rather than building up your own client base…just saying.

**People to help you**

You don't have to do all this by yourself. You cannot be the master of all the components that are required to build up a business, so what are your options? You can learn new skills and apply them to your business through courses and qualifications; you can learn by trial and error; you can have a mentor or coach to help you through the landscape of your new business set up; you can outsource some of the tasks that you find trickier, don't like, or don't have time for; or you can do a mixture of all these things.

You will need to do a skills audit to assess what you are good at, what you need training in, what you should avoid. If you were interviewing someone to run your business, what skills would you want them to be proficient in? Write these down, then give yourself an honest score out of ten to see where you need help. For each of your list of desired skills, you should be able to work out which would be your best option going forward. If you have more than one person in your team, do the same for them, so you get an idea of the skills gaps in the business.

Next you should decide how to fill these gaps. Does it need to be you who is trained? Can this be outsourced, possibly at a cost? Or could you do this yourself with the right training and push from someone? Obviously, every business is different alongside its unique owners, so it really is up to you to find and fill the skills gaps for your particular business.

| ***On your own*** |
| --- |
| Make your business skills audit to find out where your gaps are and to see if you need to engage others to help you. |

**What sort of things can be outsourced?**

The following is an idea of what you can ask (and pay for) other people to do for you in your new business. Some will be irrelevant to your business and some you will definitely want to keep to yourself.

- Payroll
- HR functions like job descriptions, sending out reference requests, etc.
- Interviewing new employees **strongly suggest you keep this on and learn how to interview if necessary, as the people you choose to work with in your business can have a marked effect on it.
- Cleaning of premises
- Caretaking of premises, including gardening
- Security of premises
- Installation and upkeep of Health and Safety functions (like fire alarm)
- Regular health and safety checks (e.g. legionella, PAT testing)
- Marketing and advertising
- Social media upkeep **be careful outsourcing this, as your 'voice' has to be right

• Bank reconciliation, bookkeeping duties
• Debt collection

You might choose how to run your business based on what you can or cannot outsource, particularly if you are still working for someone else. The above may reflect what kind of business model you have, for example, do you need staff or premises? The 'gig' economy is becoming bigger and lots of businesses are using people all over the world to fulfil tasks for them, ranging from designing a logo, to answering telephone calls, to preparing accounts for the end of the year. Your business may even be part of this new way of working. If you choose to outsource a task, you may save on staffing costs and responsibilities, but you also need to be more than super clear about what and how you want things doing, as the person (possibly in another country) will follow your instructions; if they are not clear, you only have yourself to blame.

There is a concern that using outsourcing for daily tasks may cause you to take your eye off the ball. For example, if you want someone to reconcile your banking every day, only you, not the outsourcer, will notice unusual activity or a drop in sales or income. You may use the same person to do certain tasks and so start to build up a relationship with them. This may be someone you have never met, yet you are allowing them to have direct access to your bank account. If you feel comfortable and re-assured that this is ok, go ahead. If you have the slightest doubt, keep certain tasks for yourself.

**Using a Personal Assistant (PA) or Virtual Assistant (VA)**
There are now many businesses, based in the UK and abroad, which can help you run parts of your business. In some cases, you can ask them to work on site with you, perhaps once a week, or they can access your business online and work from anywhere. The PA will need clear instructions but may take on all sorts of tasks that eat into your time, for example, organising your diary, setting up meetings, filing and sorting emails. If you cannot manage all your business tasks, you may need to get your own people in to help (see Chapter Seven), or you might use an

assistant based in another company, that you are not directly responsible for in terms of payroll, etc. You are invoiced by them or their company to carry out your tasks. As you set off on your business set up journey, it is something to think about. This book is all about planning and recognising what is or could be involved in setting up your first business and making decisions before you start which will help you later.

**Chapter Takeaways**

Even if you have a non-profit making enterprise, you will need to know your numbers. Clarifying your break-even point is crucial to enable you to work out how to price your goods and services. By thinking about this and what you will need to spend before starting your business you will be in a positive position. Banks and other lending facilities need to be confident that you understand where your money is coming from and goes to, particularly if you want to borrow some money to set yourself up.

I also recommend being very sure that your figures and business will work before you give up any externally paid employment. By starting your business small you can support yourself through your paid work whilst you get everything organised, set up and even running. This is a much less risky scenario.

**Call to action:**

Know your numbers<br>
Find your breakeven point<br>
Set up a business bank account<br>
Set up financial recording and reconciliation systems<br>
Consider outsourcing some roles

*"Buy, buy says the sign in the shop window. Why, why says the junk in the yard"*

*Paul McCartney*

# Chapter Four: Premises and Equipment

In this chapter we consider premises and whether you need them to operate your business, or whether home working is going to work better for you. You may decide to do a mixture of both. In addition, you are encouraged to consider what type of equipment you need and when you need it in order to get yourself started on your new venture.

**Do you need premises?**

Your business will determine whether you need premises and if so, what type. Firstly, you will need to decide whether premises are a requirement for you (at this stage). If you are setting up a business to teach yoga to adults, for example, you will need to secure premises before you start in order to advertise where your classes will be. In this example, you may not require a full-time space, so a shared space you can access on a regular basis may be what is required, like a church hall, for example. Using a church hall, community centre or other public building will have its advantages. Usually with this kind of premises, they are in well-known and easily accessible places. They may have parking on-site or nearby which could be a consideration. The cost per session or hour is often fixed and includes heating, lighting, etc., so no need to worry about additional bills.

Another way to share premises is to consider hot desks in an office space, which has become increasingly popular. You pay a monthly or hourly fee to be able to use the desks, and often wi-fi, in a building. The fee includes all bills and often there are bookable, private rooms for meetings, sometimes at an extra cost. With this kind of set up you get a sense of community with your business peers and can often share ideas and support each other. If you require a deeper level of support to start your business, then you could try an incubation office. This works similarly to the shared premises in terms of costs or may even be free, if it is linked to a funding body to encourage new business. The difference being that you get support and access to a variety of tools and people to help you to set up your business. Some universities have business incubators.

**Business Incubator**

Some years ago, I was studying for a Masters degree at Manchester Metropolitan University. As a business owner and entrepreneur, I was very interested when a talk was advertised about the new university business incubator. I went along and decided to set up a business there. I had been thinking for a long time about setting up a Government-backed Childcare Voucher business and decided the incubator would give me the help and confidence to move forward with this new venture. It did. I set up a limited company from this address and enjoyed the camaraderie of the people who were based there. Mutual support was genuine, and we all learned a lot from the experience. In addition, I am still in contact with many of my incubator business colleagues many years later. I would recommend that you look into this type of 'premises' if you are lucky enough to have something similar in your area.

Your premises, if you choose to have them, should reflect your business and how you want to run it:

- What kind of environment do you need?
- How far do you want to travel to your premises?
- What is local transport like, and/or parking?
- Does your working day pattern fit in with the premises?
- Where are the premises situated and how does this fit in with the image of your business?

- Are you looking for a sharing opportunity or are you better on your own?
- Are you thinking of taking your dog to work?
- Is that appropriate for your business?

**Dog Friendly Premises**

By 2009 our office based at home was proving to be problematic by being accessible to customers at all hours, so we started to look for office premises outside the home. I was very excited about 'going to work' so we drew up a list. The usual things were on it like size (we needed an office for at least 7 people at the time) and location. My Office Manager drew up a shortlist of places to visit, making a spreadsheet so we could see at a glance the advantages and disadvantages of each one. I was very taken with a newly refurbished office building with shared tea and coffee facilities, new clean offices on various floors, bookable meeting rooms and on-site parking. I got a bit carried away with this one until my Office Manager mentioned the dogs.

At home we had two well-behaved dogs who used to come into the office every day and sit under the desks. By taking on a brand-new corporate style office we would not be able to take the dogs to work. They would have to stay at home, creating issues around getting back home from the office to see to them during the day, as they were not used to being by themselves.

Eventually, we found an office that was basically like a house (and we were the only tenants) where we could take the dogs if we wanted to, so this was much more suitable. It was also closer to home, so the dogs didn't need to come to work too often. The office we chose was just right for our needs at the time. We moved in 2010 and are still there now.

**Advantages and disadvantages of home working**

You might decide it is best to work from home. Home working is exactly as it sounds, you work from home, have your home address as your business address and run all of your business interests from there. It is impossible to run some businesses from home due to their nature (like the yoga classes?), which may require a large flat space for your clients. You may however, work from home to do all but the practical aspects of your business, for example, calling clients, reconciling your bank accounts, etc. I personally do a mixture. We have an office close by, I sometimes work at one of our sites and I also work from home. I even sometimes work from abroad as all our systems are online.

In the last section I mentioned that you need your business to reflect the right image and this is where it could be tricky working from home. According to Forbes, September 2016, more than half of all businesses in the UK are run from home (possibly much higher since the world pandemic.) Yet there is still a stigma attached to working from home as it can be seen as less professional. People choose to work from home for a variety of reasons; however, these could affect the business. I remember being on the phone to a customer once when my dog decided he needed to bark at something outside. The customer asked if there was a dog with me, which there was, and I felt really embarrassed by the situation. On another occasion at around 10 o'clock at night time, a customer called our home phone, thinking it was one of my children wanting a lift home I picked up. I found it was a customer, who was unfortunately a little the worse for wine, demanding that I book her child into one of my services the next day. This and other stories I could relate about home working were what made me take the plunge and get an office outside the home.

**Something to think about:**

What image are you trying to portray?
Does your work environment reflect that?

If you do want to work from home, you will have to separate your home from your business, preferably in a physical way as well as mentally. I found that when my business was based at home, there was always something to do, check up on or finish. When I had a separate office, I had to leave it at some point and go home, leaving all those jobs, checks and emails until the next day. Others may find it difficult to comprehend that you are working when you are at home and this is one of the biggest complaints from home workers. People assume you are available for them when you are at the house which may cause friction. Therefore, if you are working from home, think carefully about your workload and how you let people know what you are doing. Some try to look after children when they are working from home and again this can be problematic. You end up not doing either job well if you are not careful about how you allocate your time.

Working from home, however, can save money. You will need to consider where to have meetings and appointments if this is part of your business. It may not be appropriate to invite people to your house for a meeting. There are lots of small spaces that you can rent out by the hour, for example rooms in office buildings, meeting rooms in hotels and restaurants. There is usually a cost involved for these, or you could just meet someone for a coffee in a café, which is possibly the most cost effective. If you are using other people's businesses to have your meetings, a café for example, be mindful of their business and how long you are spending there. It's not very fair to sit for three hours having a meeting with a single cup of coffee each.

Another implication to consider if you are working from home is the confidentiality of your work, if this is relevant. Also, you will always be at work; only you will be able to battle with that one. As I said earlier, working from home was great for a while for me but as the business got larger it became impossible in the space. Also, I would always find something that needed doing (at whatever time of the day or night!).

**Premises preparation**

Whether you have decided to work from home or away from home in your new business, you will want to get your premises ready for your new venture. Although we will look at online and offline businesses later, you will probably need an internet connection or access to the internet in your premises. If you are having to have this installed, remember it can take a number of weeks to organise and set up which may affect when you begin trading. Similarly, if you need a landline, this will take some time to organise.

Luckily, nowadays, there are alternatives, for example a cellular laptop which has as much data on it as you require (purchased or on contract). This could be a cheap way of spreading the cost of some equipment and solve a data usage problem, short or long term. Similarly, you could use a VOIP (Voice Over Internet Protocol) phone instead of acquiring a landline. Using your mobile may be convenient but does it reflect the professionalism that you want to achieve? If not, you could use a landline number and get it sent through to your mobile, or skipping back to the last chapter, you could employ someone to take calls for you. This service enables the phone to be answered by a human and they reroute the call to you, if necessary; they will also screen the nuisance calls.

How will you prepare your working environment in terms of decoration? Do you need specific furniture? If you are working from home, does your environment feel like a work environment or does it feel like your spare bedroom?
I think there's a lot to be said for making your work environment feel business-like, even if you have to clear it away each night and set it up again the next day. In my opinion, it helps you to think differently, allowing your brain to work out this is now work and not home. If you get your office 'ready' you get your mindset ready.

**A new beginning**
Some years ago, I had to go back into one of my businesses to manage it myself. This was not something I was looking forward to. My role had changed and it felt like I was taking a step back by taking on this position. The way I dealt with this was to go to the business one weekend and to re-decorate the office where I would be spending most of my time. With a quick lick of paint and a change round of furniture, I made the

office seem quite different. It was all I needed to make me feel that this was a new beginning and not more of the 'same old, same old'.

Obviously, you don't have to redecorate to make your workspace feel conducive to working. You can add a large wall calendar, a few stationery items and storage facilities to make any work area, at home or in a new space, feel like your office. If you have people who come into your office regularly, make sure that anything on display is representative of your work values. For example, you may have a white board with customer details on it. Is this ok in terms of confidentiality? If not, think of another way of storing your information - a filing cabinet holds lots of papers and files. If you have items that you need to store in hard copy files, consider using a filing cabinet, or a smaller cabinet with two rather than four drawers, or a desk drawer with a built-in filing space. Obviously, storing any data securely online is the safest way.

If your office looks good and is tidy(ish), then you can probably get to work straight away when you access your workspace. Of course, you may be the sort of person who prefers working with a laptop on your knee, in which case your workspace will be your laptop, so you should probably aim to keep that tidy too.

**An offline or an online business**

What kind of business will you be running? If your business lends itself to being run exclusively online you will possibly be able to make savings on your premises, as you will not need a shop, workspace or office. However, be mindful that although the sale of your goods may be online, the actual business of getting those goods from your online store to the customer may have to take place offline. You may still require premises for administration purposes, even if you use a fulfilment company that sends out products on your behalf. You need to think carefully about choosing this route, as this will affect your breakeven for the products you sell and may even make the business unviable.

If you look at the news, you will know that many high street retailers are closing their shops, due to online competition. Another main reason for high street closures is that rents and rates are very high in town and city centres. You may, however, be able to bag a bargain on a deal for premises due to this. No-one wants to see the high street empty of shops and life, so councils are offering decent incentives to people to open stores within shopping areas. To find out more about this you would need to contact your local council to see if there are any such incentives in your area.

If you need to store and package items yourself, to fulfil your own online orders, is there a post office close by, a courier service, or will you need to pay for warehousing and shipping costs? If this is the case, you need to find out more about the exact costs of these, as this will affect your profits. You will still need a business address even if you are online. Most people want to know that there is a physical address to send items back to or send a complaint letter to in the event of having a concern. An address also gives people confidence in you and trust starts to develop. By choosing to be online with your business you choose a new set of circumstances to navigate – that of visibility. How will people find you? How do they know what you sell? Once on your website, it's easy but how are they going to get to the website in the first place? In Chapter Six we cover branding and marketing.

What about if you have a people business? Where will you 'meet' people? How can you build up the trust if no-one has actually seen or met you? You may need to think about video calling and shared meetings through social media or video conferencing. Although this sounds ideal as it is online, there is a lot of work that goes into each meeting before-hand, particularly if the meeting *is* the business, for example, in a coaching business. The meeting should be recorded for the client so your 'work' and their value will be recorded for reference. Where will you set up the meeting? What technology will you need to do so and what training will you require to put everything into practice?

I know there's a lot of questions to answer, points to be made and thought about but now is the best time to do this. There's no point in you offering a service then finding you can't deliver it, are not skilled enough or don't have the right equipment to follow it through. That would make you look unprofessional and you would lose the client's trust (and probably the client as well!).

> **TIP**
> Consider the responsibilities of premises carefully; there are many hidden costs, like engaging a solicitor, surveyors, condition reports.

**Getting Premises**

You may not be in the financial position to buy premises just yet, particularly if you are just starting out, so leasing premises is a great way to allow you to start your business. There are advantages and disadvantages to leasing premises.

**Advantages:**

1. You can be very visible, choosing a high street location
2. You will know exactly what your rent and rates will be each month so you can budget
3. You can estimate your utility bill usage for your budget by asking the current/previous tenants how much gas, electricity and water they use
4. You will have your own space (not to be underestimated!)
5. You will probably (check lease) be able to make minor improvements to fit in with your brand
6. The outside can be used as an advertising space (subject to planning permission)
7. You can start to become part of the community you serve.

**Disadvantages of leasing premises can be:**

1. Costs - these can be very high to set up the lease in the first place as this is a legal document, therefore you need to take legal advice
2. You may be bound by the lease for years, problematic if your business closes down or if you need different premises, or if you

are signed up to a short lease, where the landlord can exercise his right to terminate the agreement
3. You will probably be on a full repairing lease which means if anything goes wrong with the building you have to fix it at your expense
4. You will have to pay to have a dilapidation report done at the beginning and end of your contract. This is like an inventory of the state of the building and spaces you will occupy.
5. You must pay your rent and rates even when the business is not bringing in enough funds to pay them, so need to budget for that.
6. You may find it difficult to get out of a lease once you have signed it. You may have to assign it over to someone else if you want to leave.

Business Rates for premises may be free, depending on the local council, the size of your premises and business. At time of writing there is a rates relief for businesses which often accounts for the whole rates payable on small business premises…something less to worry about.

**Beware Repairs**
We rent a building for one of our businesses, inherited with a roof continually in a state of disrepair. We have patched it up many times and recently had to pay out thousands of pounds to keep ourselves dry when the leaks got really bad. I would love to be able to claim this back from somewhere, but I know that part of the lease is to keep the building in a well-maintained state, so we just have to pay for repairs like this along the way. As we have about ten years left on the lease, I made a calculation; rather than getting small short-term repairs done continually, we have just decided to have a major repair done with guarantees which, although expensive, will hopefully cost us less in the long run.

So, repairs on buildings are something that you need to look out for. Lastly on premises and leases, you may be asked to provide a deposit up front, as a security against you not paying the rent, or not attending to maintenance on the building so you will need to budget for that as well.

**Equipment required to run your business**

> **TIP**
> Hiring equipment rather than buying helps with costs, plus phones, laptops, etc. – are automatically kept up to date

In the last chapter you were asked to think about what kind of equipment you require and whether you could manage by renting some or making do, as you try to save money in setting up your new business. Now it's time to take this to the next stage and do two jobs in one. I suggest you make a list of the equipment you need to get your business going. On one side write your list and on the other side where you could get it from and how much it costs. For example, left side says 'computer', right side says 'own' (lent to business). As you can see, there is no cost involved in this one. Next example might be, left side says 'filing cabinet, 4-drawer', right hand side says '£40.00 second hand from Bargain shop'. If you write down the condition of the items as well, you are starting to build up a resource list and inventory for your business.

You can make a separate list for things that you haven't got yet, like a printer, but you know that you saw the perfect one priced at £45.00. You have now started to make a resource request or wish list. Always put down the prices, if possible, for two reasons; firstly, it makes you do some research to find out the best place to buy the item and secondly, you know exactly how much you will need to save or earn to buy the new item, which can be very motivating. You can put your resource lists onto a spreadsheet, colouring them in or highlighting as you add equipment to your business. You may be able to claim back for most of the expenses for your business as well, so it's useful to have your inventory, including the condition of the items.

***On your own***
Make an equipment list, which doubles up as a wish list and an inventory.

Did you know that you can rent office furniture? It obviously depends on the kind of premises you are going for (if any) but it's worth looking into if money is tight but you want customers to visit you. You can also check out eBay or local sellers for second-hand items which will be as good as new. In our office we are still sitting at the same desks that we got (free on collection) approximately 16 years ago. They still look good and do their job, so why change them? We had to factor in the cost of hiring a van but this more than made up for getting free furniture.

**Set yourself a budget**
A few years ago, we were renovating a property to sell which was part of one of our businesses. Our tight budget meant we needed to sell as quickly as possible after the refurbishment. In order to do this, we wanted to dress the property so that it looked good. I allocated a budget of £400.00 to do this. It was brilliant fun. Because we didn't need to live in the property and the furniture was just to make it look like a house, we did not have to add in all the knick-knacks that houses often accumulate, just the basics. I bought fireplace surrounds, mirrors and beds. Curtains and bedding were borrowed from family members. We acquired a three-piece suite and coffee tables, a dining table and 6 chairs, bedside cabinets and a couple of wardrobes. Everything was second hand or borrowed. We just stuck to the basic items for each room and hey presto, the house looked lovely. When the house sold, we were able to give most of what we had accrued to a charity specialising in large furniture items and I definitely had lots of fun sourcing the furniture and staying under budget.

It can be fun to make do, so save your 'equipment money' for systems that you need to help you to run the business. As a minimum, you will probably need a website with

hosting and a telephone. Using Microsoft office suite or something similar will
probably fulfil your needs until you require something more sophisticated.

> **TIP**
> Beg, 'steal' and borrow what equipment you can to get your business started.

**Chapter Takeaways**

Deciding on working from business premises or from home may be an easy decision for you to make, due to the nature of your business. However, if you need to consider the advantages and disadvantages, this chapter will have given you some food for thought; from considering whether or not to take on premises, or work from home to which kind of premises would be most suitable and reflective of your business. You can always change your mind about your premises situation and move from home to an office environment if you so wish once the business is generating enough money to pay for this expense.

**Call to action:**

Decide whether you need premises
Home or away?
Choose a premises which reflects on the business
Even when working online, you need somewhere to work from
Consider the right premises type for you and your business
Choose a working environment which will help you to work effectively
Think about inventive ways to gain equipment

*"Ideas are easy. Implementation is hard."*

*Guy Kawasaki*

# Chapter Five: Paperwork

**The way we do things around here**

When you start a new job you usually have an induction period. You learn all the basic things about the role, health and safety requirements, their expectations about your work, your conduct, dress code, language, everything. You hear stories from the company, about individuals who work there and who used to work there, what to avoid with whom and when not to bother such and such…you get the idea. Well, in your own business you get none of that.

You make all the rules. You become the story.

Everything will be down to you to set up in the way you want to do it…and breathe!! It doesn't have to be the onerous task it sounds. Naturally, the story of the business will evolve as you work in it, trial things, change things and adapt. New people will bring new ideas and not just people who work in your business, but also people who come into contact with you and your business. Embrace this, as it is one of the few times that you may actually have complete control over the direction of a project. I agree it is a little scary to think there is no one to say no, no-one to shake their head at your ideas and no-one to pick up on your mistakes. There is also no-one to ask for permission and that can be the most liberating thing when you discover it.

**Parent Manual**

Those of you who are parents may relate to this. I have two children. I was a teacher when I had my first child so was quite used to looking after and educating children. However, when my son was born, I felt quite unprepared for the responsibility, even though I had major responsibilities in my job and even though I had been preparing for this for the best part of 9 months. The morning someone comes to your hospital bed and says you can go home and take the baby with you is a terrifying moment. You have wanted to do this for so long, but reality is very different. Will he be safe? What if I can't get him to sleep, feed, stop crying? How will I know what each cry means? What is it going to be like?

No one gives you a baby manual on the way out; you just have to figure it out based on your own learning, those around you who are willing to help and probably, mostly, your gut instinct. You are on your own.

Your new role of being a business owner is similar; you are in control; you can make your own rules. You can tell yourself exactly how things are done around here. You should see this as an opportunity, one which often passes others by. You can do your own induction and make your own rules. These will be based on your values and what you see as important. When you looked at your business plan earlier you were asked to think about your values and the reasons behind them. Your values help decide on your mission statement and what is important to you. As we start this chapter it is a good time to reflect on what is important to you as, hopefully, the procedures and policies you put in place now will stand you in good stead for years to come.

In our businesses we check our policies annually to make sure they still fit our values and are still relevant. Many of the policies we have, particularly in the childcare business, are little changed from the originals almost 20 years ago, because our core values have not changed in all those years. What was important to us as individuals and as a company 20 years ago is still important today.

**Keeping Records**

Every business must keep certain records. Most businesses are asked to keep all financial records for about 6 years in case HMRC wish to inspect them to check, not only on you but on your accountant's practice as well. Beyond that, you may have industry records and standards to adhere to. In my childcare business we have to keep records for much longer, for insurance and regulation purposes. The requirement to maintain these kinds of records is dictated to us by external bodies and there is nothing we can do about it. We have to follow these rules or risk huge penalties and sometimes, potential imprisonment for not complying. So that's cleared that one up. We should all keep the statutory records we are supposed to for the minimum required length of time. But what other records are important to our business?

Most businesses will have records or paperwork on the following:

- How the business is run
- Suppliers
- Employees
- Customers
- Contacts
- Premises details
- Finance
- Health and safety
- Marketing
- Meetings
- Ideas and plans
- Passwords

**Why do we need to keep records?**

We need accountability and to know what is happening in our business, our records and paperwork will show this. We need to file all our paperwork in one place if possible. Either a sturdy, lockable filing cabinet, if you need to use paper, or (and preferably) an online filing system which is linked to the cloud so that storage, access and security of material is not a problem.

The two main things to remember with records is a) they should be easily accessible and b) they should not exist only in one person's head, even if it's only you in the business.

**Once upon a time in a business long, long ago…**

…there was an owner who had started her business from scratch. She knew how each and every part of the business worked. She knew the names of all the staff and clients, numbering many hundreds. She understood how everything worked and was a font of knowledge on every aspect of the business.

Her job was often interrupted by people asking questions. Where is the …? What does this mean? How do we do that? Who knows about …? Why does that happen? How much is …?

One day she felt ill so couldn't come to work. The others at work still asked the questions but no-one knew the answers, so they rang the unwell owner at home.

When the owner came into work the next day she talked to the staff. 'I have all the answers in my head and you don't know the answers,'' she said. 'What can be done?'

Luckily, her colleagues were very clever and suggested a system be developed to get everything out of the owner's head into a file so they could answer the questions themselves. This was a great success and the owner and all the staff were very content and they all lived happily ever after.

Not sure who that fairy story is based on…! But we can all learn a lot from the tale. By having everything in ~~my~~ her head, the owner was doing two things: She was disempowering her team and making more work for herself.

Using a system to store all your 'answers' is a great idea and one which you can think about now at the very start of your journey.

Most people, including myself, have stumbled across ways of doing things as they go along. However, you are in a unique position to think about this right from the beginning.

**The perfect business**
After about 6 years of running a business, I decided to add in another one. That business was the perfect format. I had made all my mistakes with the first one, so I was in a position to learn from them and set up the new business exactly as I wanted to. I still regard it as my textbook business as it was set up with all the knowledge of the first one.

**Storage online**
People setting up their businesses nowadays have been given a gift. The internet has made business so much easier to do and to access. I recommend using an online, cloud-based system to store your 'business'. I know for some people this can be a worry, as you are concerned about the cloud going down and losing information as a result. When I was making the big move from paper to online, I had the same worries and was told this by an expert: 'If the cloud goes down there's no need to worry about your business or information as we will probably all be dead'. Sobering thought. I think the sentiment behind the statement was that if the internet was 'broken,' it may be for a bad reason that everything was lost. We are not immune to cyber-attacks though and such events make the news when large companies are held to ransom over their data. Also, there have been data breaches and again these have made the news. I think you have to put those events into perspective. There have been plane crashes where people have died, not just had their addresses exposed, yet we still all travel by plane. The reason we hear about data breaches is because they are unusual and there are ways to mitigate against being cyber attacked. I think the positives of storing information online far outweighs the negatives.

You will need to protect all your devices by installing anti-virus software. Protect your systems and equipment with passwords. Know who knows how to access your systems and be vigilant about changing codes and passwords when they leave. Do your own checks on people who are accessing your systems. We do a Disclosure and Barring Check (DBS) on all our staff who work in the childcare business. This is a requirement of working with children. However, we also do the same check on anyone who works in our office. This is because they have access to sensitive information, including accessing our systems. If you are going to employ someone to manage your finances, you may want to know that they do not have a criminal record or you could unknowingly be inviting a criminal (fraud is a criminal act) into your business. Rather than getting too worried about putting things online look at it this way; you wouldn't leave your house unlocked so why would you leave your business unlocked?

You will be less likely to be the victim of an attack if you have online, cloud-based storage for your important documents and in addition, you will be able to access them from anywhere in the world, so no need to be bound to an office or work environment.

**Held to Ransom**

Before we moved everything online, and the reason we did, we suffered a cyber-attack. We arrived at the office one morning to find the computer had a message saying it had been hacked and we had to pay an amount of bitcoins (I can't actually remember how much but it was in the thousands) into an account to release our computer or they would delete everything.

There were two problems with this. Firstly, I had no idea how to pay a ransom in bitcoins! Secondly, as our computer was inaccessible, it was stopping us from working. We called in our regular IT guy who took the computer away and managed to mostly get rid of the virus. Instead of it making us feel that we were not safe, we looked for ways to protect our business and the information we held to make it even safer and less susceptible to any problems. That was when we had one of our biggest business shifts, which was to go online with everything.

We currently use a couple of online storage platforms, like Dropbox and Google Docs, to store our records safely as a result of this incident. I use the larger companies, knowing that they have teams of people whose role is to constantly keep out the attackers, so I feel safe they are doing that job well and that my information is safe. The downside of not using online facilities and storage is time. From where I am sitting now, I can access my bank accounts, write this book, check how my businesses are doing, keep up with social media and emails…the list goes on. Imagine having to do all those things face to face. We are truly lucky to be living in these times.

***On your own***
Deciding on where you store paperwork should be your next issue. Will it be on paper in a filing cabinet or online?

**Using Systems in your business**
We have already established that you need to think about your systems right from the beginning and I have a tried and tested way of working which you can adopt, if it suits you, right from the inception of your business. I call it the Three Folder System.

The Three Folder System uses (you guessed it!) just three online folders (you can do this on paper if you like as well), to store and sort all your business information. It's a bit like a business in a box.

By keeping everything to do with your business in just three distinct areas, you will find it easy to locate items and records; everything has a logical place and it keeps it all tidy. The Three Folders are Paperwork, Finance and People. Everything you need will fit into one of these folders. Each of these folders has subfolders but the beauty is in how tidy the system looks.

Your business needs will determine what exactly you put into each folder, so if you are not yet employing people (People Folder) you may have only included your own job description and a file with your own details, and your client list. I think it's important to set up your business systems with all the components, as if it is a larger concern, for two reasons. Firstly, you set up a complete system, with no gaps, and secondly, you have to think about how this system will look eventually when your business has grown. So, you are starting with the end in mind – Stephen Covey.

Each of the Three Folders is divided into subfolders, an example of which is below to give you an idea.

1

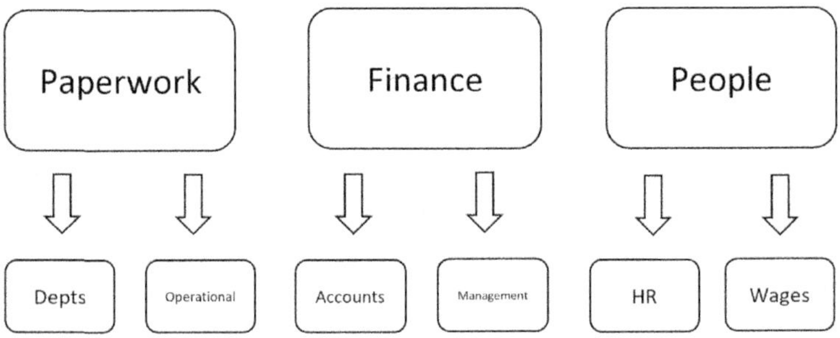


To make your own Three Folder System, decide what to put into each folder and subfolder so it fits your specific business. Draw out your folder map onto paper, to get things in the right order. I use colours to make it look more interesting. It is one of the few things I also print, so I and others can see at a glance where items should be stored or retrieved from. By using the map, your whole business is in one place. This simple organisation of files makes your business look and feel professional.

**TIP**

For an extra bit of professionalism, use a strong colour for each of the three folders at the top of your map and lighter/darker shades of the same colour for files within each folder, e.g. if 'Paperwork' is blue, make the subfolders beneath lighter blues.

**Setting up your 'office handbook'**

Whether you have an office or not I recommend you consider setting up an 'office handbook'. An office handbook is an invaluable resource for your business as you set up. It will also come in handy as your business grows to help train others or eventually if you want to sell your business. It contains everything you and anyone else needs to know about your business and how it operates. At this stage of your business life cycle it is easy to start documenting information in the office handbook for use later, whilst you are devising systems, deciding on suppliers and so on. You may as well take a little bit longer and document what and why you are doing it, therefore starting to devise your office handbook.

Linked to your Three Folder System, the office handbook is an online version of your business blueprint. It contains all the 'know-how' and 'how-to' of your business. For example, we have a software system to sign children in and out of our childcare settings which we developed in-house. There is no manual from a manufacturer. If there was, part of the office handbook would simply be a link to that manufacturer's notes. As it is, we have our own version of this which covers:

- What the system does and who uses it
- Passwords to get into the system
- The user experience and how they access the system (step by step)
- Office user experience and how to access various parts of the system (step by step)
- A training manual for managers to use with new staff
- Trouble shooting pages for admin to access
- Contact details of the system developers in case we can't put things right ourselves
- Access to the website from a user's point of view which can be shared with them
- Access into the back end of the system for admin users to make adjustments

You can see how each step in using the system is broken down into smaller parts to enable everyone who needs it, to access the right part. The detailed record stored in the office handbook is useful as a guide, very much like a manufacturer's product guide but specifically about your business. The test comes when a new person accesses the system. If they can do so by following the user guides successfully, the office handbook has done its job. If they find that bits are missing or could be made clearer, there is room for improvement. When you set up your office handbook you must add and change things as they happen to keep an updated version. By doing this you and anyone else will always be working on the best version.

This can be applied to everything needed to run your business. It comes down to details, such as how you want people to answer the phone. Do you want them to say their name on answering or do you have a little script? We always answer the phone within three rings and say good afternoon, (business name), (person answering's name), speaking. So, at Coaches Unlimited, it goes like this, 'Good afternoon, Coaches Unlimited, Terri speaking.' Did you notice that I said that we answer within three rings? That is one of our company targets. I like callers to get our attention straight away.

Who writes the office handbook? Everyone. If you are a sole trader, unfortunately you are everyone at the moment so it will be down to you. If you have other people working with you then it should be the person who best knows the system or procedure you are documenting. Their copy can then be tested by any newbie who comes along as they try to follow the instructions laid out. This office handbook doubles up as a training manual, so it's worth spending time getting it right. If the systems don't work or there are bits missing, new staff should add them in. It is a working document.

**Health and safety**

Whatever kind of industry you are in, you will have to consider, to some degree, health and safety issues. Even if you don't have people working with you in an office, you will have certain rules to follow regarding health and safety. Firstly, you may need public liability insurance. You will need this even if you just do an exhibition event at a church hall (unless the venue covers everyone exhibiting). You need to consider what you are offering to the public and how, then seek advice as to whether or what kind of insurance you will need to have.

In addition, you need to consider people's privacy and their data. You may need to gain a compliance certificate from the ICO or Information Commission Office (don't worry it's not as bad as it sounds). The ICO want to know what data you are collecting and how you are using and storing it. You complete a questionnaire online and this lets you know whether you need to register with them. The fee is under £50.00 per year for a small business, paid annually, at time of writing, so it's not a huge amount to stay on the right side of the law. In some businesses you have to display both your ICO certificate and your insurance certificate, so be mindful of this as well.

For some types of business, you also need to be aware of the Health and Safety at Work Act depending on where you operate from. If you are in a shared office, you can probably find one of their posters up on the wall. It's a good idea to read this through just so that you know what it is about. If you prepare food in your business, you may need to be inspected by the local environmental health officer. They come to look at your premises and your food preparation practice, including keeping paperwork up to date. They will issue you with a report about your site and a certificate with a number on it. 5 is the best rating and 1 is the lowest. When you go into a restaurant you will be able to see the food hygiene rating of the establishment as the certificate has to be displayed.

If you are not compliant with Health and Safety regulations your business could be closed or you could be prosecuted or sent to prison if things are really bad. That is why it's important to make sure you have adequate insurance in place, if required. If you run your business from a building where you are the responsible person, you will also be responsible for gas and electricity checks, water checks, including testing for legionella, and building maintenance checks. You may decide that this is one area of your business that you outsource to a specialist company. You are still ultimately responsible, but it might give you peace of mind if specialists are taking on this area of your responsibility.

> **Something To Think About:**
>
> Consider all the legal issues which you may come across for your business type to make sure you are compliant

Apart from the Health and Safety and data protection compliance there are a few more issues that you may need to think about. If applicable, you also need to comply with employment law. This starts when you begin to advertise for staff and continues into their employment. Employees have certain rights, for example, you will need to ensure you are not discriminating in any way in a job advertisement, at interview or in work. In the chapter on staffing, you will find out about the procedures of employing people in more detail.

Your premises lease, as previously discussed is a legal document and one which you need to comply with. As part of that you will probably be asked to display your insurance certificate.

> **TIP**
> Become a terms and conditions ninja. If you can, get into the habit of reading all the small print. You'll be surprised what's there! Most people don't so it immediately sets you apart and is good practice. After all, you are signing to say that you agree.

As far as your paperwork is concerned, all the health and safety and legal issues should be filed in your Three Folder system. In the case of items to be displayed, keep a scanned copy in your filing system for completeness. Label everything carefully. There's nothing more frustrating and time consuming than having to search for documents because they are not clearly labelled.

Regarding your own terms and conditions, you will need to devise these and make them available to your clients. Think carefully about what your expectations are and whether these are reasonable. Maybe have a look at other people's terms and conditions in your business industry to see what they are expecting from their clients. If you need to change your terms and conditions you must inform anyone who has already signed a contract with you, giving them the opportunity to withdraw from the new agreement without penalty. You will need to issue new Ts and Cs to your clients well before the changeover to the new terms, unless your contract with them is a fixed term in which case, when your contract with them ends, so do the terms and conditions associated with that contract. It may be wise to seek legal advice if you are in any doubt or want someone to check over your paperwork to ensure that you are compliant and fair.

**Chapter Takeaways**

Getting all your paperwork in order may seem like a chore if you are a creative person. But the importance of getting this sorted and clear right at the beginning of your business journey cannot be emphasised enough. It puts you in a strong position if you know where everything is and if everything has a place.

**Call to action**

Decide on what paperwork your new business will require.
Think about how to store your paperwork.
Develop your own Three Folder System, or use something similar.
Put together your office handbook or manual to start your 'how to' systems.

*"In every success story you will find someone who has made a courageous decision."*

*Peter F Drucker*

# Chapter Six: Marketing and Branding

People often get into a panic when they think about marketing and branding, wrongly assuming that it is a bottomless money pit. It doesn't have to be. However, sometimes with marketing it does take time (and time usually means money, although not always.) If you have some time now whilst you are thinking about setting up your business, start to develop your marketing plan and spend time, not money.

Branding is not the same as marketing. Marketing is about actively seeking to engage people so they become your clients and customers. Branding is about your identity as a company (or individual).

**Your Marketing Plan**

Every business needs to bring in money to make a profit and to be able to call itself a business. You will need to set out a plan of action to help you identify your potential customers and to look at how best to make them customers. Traditional marketing routes cover things like leaflet drops, a website for the product or service, adverts in newspapers and magazines, advertorials (where you write a piece about your product), testimonials online and so on. You may, however, find that the best route to your intended market is through social media, which is becoming an increasingly popular way to advertise, as the platforms can differentiate between groups of people and provide you with targeted groups to more accurately aim your advertising.

We can learn a lot from the big advertisers as well. One Christmas there was a strange advert on primary television channels at peak time. All it said was the word 'Hello'. The singer Adele had been quiet for some time and this was a brilliant strategy for marketing her new album. It caused intrigue and left people guessing what it was about.

Other big advertisers are the large stores who now put out a Christmas advert which is more like a short film. People have started looking forward to them and they are cause for a lot of discussion. You don't have to spend thousands of pounds on television advertising, but you can learn from them. By using anticipation and build up as part of their campaign, they get people talking. Job done.

If people are talking about your products and services, you are halfway there. You just have to make sure that what they are saying is positive. The big stores are catering for the masses, but it will probably be the case that you need your advertising and marketing to be more niche and cater for a more manageable audience.

**Who is your target audience?**

You need to be clear about who will buy your product or service. For example, if you are going to be selling vegan 'sausage' rolls, how can you identify the people who will buy them? You would be wasting money advertising to meat eaters. However, you would do well advertising in places where non-meat eaters congregate like vegan blogs or recipe websites.

Where does your best customer hang out and what do they read? How do you reach them? To identify your target audience, it's a good idea to make up a fictional character who would be willing to buy your product. To do this you decide on many things about them such as the list below. Some people call this an avatar exercise, others call it a persona. I am going to call it an avatar for the purpose of the exercise.

• Name – By giving your Avatar a name you start to make them real. Don't worry if the name doesn't come to you straight away, you can always add it in later, when you know more about their personality.

• Description including Age – Actually describe the physical appearance of your Avatar, height, weight, gender. Try to really see the person in your mind's eye. Some people scour the internet or magazines for a stock photo of someone (not famous and no-one familiar to you), to become their avatar and that's ok as well. If you have an actual photo, then you can start to see this person as real.

• Personality traits - The more you can add the better. Regard it as building up a character for a fiction book.

• Relationship status – Are they married, in a relationship or single? Are they happy in their relationships? Don't forget relationships with family members, colleagues and others to build up your picture.

• Family members – Who is part of their family? Are they a parent, brother or sister, a grandparent? Where do family members live, close by or far away? What are their relationships like with these people? If you are setting up a coaching or counselling service this may be an important consideration for your business.

• Job or work - What do they do? Have they always done that? How do they find it? Are they happy doing their current work? What frustrates them if anything?

• Education and childhood/background - How did they get to where they are now?

• Values and beliefs – What does your avatar think? This is not just about their religious values although it could be if that is fundamental to their personality. This is more about their views on the world and how they fit into it. What excites them, what annoys them? Do they fight for any causes?

• Hobbies and interests – What do they do in their spare time? How much spare time do they have? Are they unusual hobbies or run of the mill?

• Challenges they face in their everyday life - This could be from anything, e.g. work related, family related, values related. Don't forget that not everyone has huge challenges and that's ok too if that's their profile.

• Why they would want or need your products – A bit more nitty-gritty now. What is it in their life that has led you to believe they would be the ideal candidate for your product or service?

• Friends or groups and societies they are part of who they could share this information with – Who will they tell? What social media platforms do they belong to? Remember this avatar is the best person for your product or service so the people they interact with hopefully will be interested too. If your person is a raving fan of your business, they will encourage others to be too.

**Ways of marketing**

With the information you have above about your target audience or avatar you can now turn your attention to how to market your product with them in mind. Will your avatar be on Facebook or Instagram, for example and is this a good way to reach them? Or are they a newspaper reader or a member of a specific group which takes a monthly subscription magazine?

You need to see your marketing plan like a business plan and follow a format in order to set yourself achievable goals and targets for marketing. This way you will be able to track your marketing progress and measure whether your campaigns are successful.

**Return on Investment (ROI)**

You will need to work out your return on investment, when looking at your marketing budget. This is basically like a break-even point with a difference, as you have to look at the lifetime value of one customer. Let's work through an example.

If you make and sell vegan 'sausage' rolls (Vrolls) as your business model and have worked out that you need to sell them at £1.50 to make a £1.00 profit per roll.

If you spend £50.00 on advertising, then you will need to sell 50 more rolls to make up for your (£50.00) advertising budget.

So, you need an extra 50 customers buying one Vroll each. However, when those customers eat the Vrolls they become fans of your product and tell their friends (they may do this through word of mouth, testimonials or social media). In addition to this, the new customers start to buy the Vrolls each week.

Quite quickly you have made your money back on advertising because the new customers are buying the product, you may also have developed some lifetime customers. This has been a good return on your original outlay of £50.00 for advertising. I have obviously used a simple example and simple numbers, but I hope you get the idea.

**Radio Advert**

A long time ago I decided to run an advertising campaign on a local radio station. It entailed having a jingle made with voice actors reading from a script to promote a newly opened day nursery. As part of the package, I was interviewed on the radio station, talking about my nursery, the staff and a little bit about why we set it up.

The following week we got a phone call from a parent who had heard the interview. She came to see the nursey and said that after listening to our jingle advert many times, and having heard the interview, she wanted to see the nursery for herself.
Her child was quite shy, and she was worried about him being in a day care environment. However, she decided to put her child into our nursery.

Over the next few years, we had four of her children come through the nursery. That was a good return on investment. The advertising costs for the radio campaign were more than covered by having a new full-time child in our nursery, the icing on the cake being the other children from the same family that joined us, in addition to her telling her friends about us.

**What do you need to put on your marketing plan?**
You can set out an easy-to-use marketing plan by following 5 simple steps which I call the 5 stars marketing plan.

Star 1. Your overall aims and objectives
Star 2. Your strategy for how you are going to achieve these
Star 3. Who will be responsible?
Star 4. How will this be tracked and monitored?
Star 5. Evaluation of success

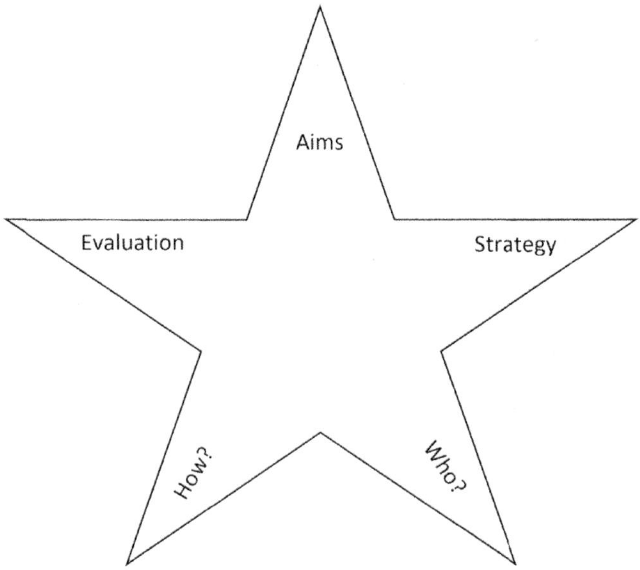


Let's work through an example of the 5 Stars Marketing Plan

**Your overall aims and objectives**
What do you want to achieve with this marketing plan? For example, the first one you write might be as simple as getting yourself noticed. So, your aim would be to set up a website.

Your strategy for doing this will possibly entail the following:
1. Buy a domain name linked to your business and decide where this will be hosted. You may find you can get a deal for both, including an email address at your chosen domain name. Think

about your business name and what people may be searching for on the internet to find you and your products and services.
2. Learn how to build up a website (using the how to guides and videos provided by the host?)
3. Build your website
4. Link it all up to go live and then
5. Launch

**A word about time**
I have deliberately separated all these sections rather than say build a website and put it online, as you will need to think about the timing of each of the above parts. For example, you will know your own timetable and how much time you have to spend on this. You will also know your own skill levels and be able to estimate how long each bit will take. If you are a complete beginner with website building, you will need a longer time in the learning phase and so on, or to engage someone else.

Think about how long you will need to spend on each task and mark it on your action plan. You may also note when you want a certain task doing by. If this is the case, be as specific as possible. It's amazing how concentrated your mind becomes when you are specific with your plan.

**Who is responsible?**
Next you will need to think about who can do each part of the tasks in your strategy. It might be mostly you, but it's important to decide who is responsible. If it is another person, make sure they know they are responsible and approximately when you need the task completing by.

**Tracking and monitoring**
Tracking your progress is very important. If you track your tasks and how they are going, it gives you a sense of achievement and momentum. If you have written your marketing plan on a spreadsheet, you can use the traffic light system to track your progress (see Chapter Two on Planning). This is particularly useful if you are going to share it with someone else, as you can both see at a glance the colour of the task and therefore, where

each part of the strategy is up to. You don't necessarily need to do everything in the order that you wrote it; some tasks naturally follow on and others may stand alone. If you only have time for a small task, do that one. Everything adds up to make a whole.

**Evaluation of Success**

It is important to evaluate the success of any advertising and marketing initiative. It will give you an idea of how things are going, whether you have a good Return on Investment (ROI), and whether something has not worked. If this is the case, it is an opportunity to examine how you can make improvements.

The best measures of success are quantifiable, i.e. if you aim to get 100 more connections on LinkedIn, you know when you have achieved this as you will have 100 more connections. Other strategies are less measurable, but you should try to quantify them. For example, in the case of a new website, the evaluation of success may be that by a certain date you will have your new website live. If you get to that date and it is online, you have succeeded. If you find you need more time to do something, there is nothing wrong with altering your goals and aims. However, be mindful that you cannot continually avoid working on and achieving your strategy aims.

**Making a social media content plan**

When considering the marketing of your business you will probably want to use social media. Firstly, you will need to decide which platforms are best to access your ideal customers or clients. That is why you were asked to do the avatar exercise earlier. You know exactly where your ideal customer will be online.

Each social media platform engages a different type of user and the user experience is different with each. I shall not go into details here about each social media platform and how this works. If you need clarification, do some research to find out what each one offers users and how this will fit into your marketing plan.

On most platforms you can pay for targeted advertising and every platform knows a surprising amount about their user demographics. If, for example, your avatar is a certain age and demographic, you can tailor your social media adverts directly to people who are similar. You have to pay for this type of advertising, so will need to check the ROI for your business type and whether this is a good idea, particularly when you compare it to other forms of marketing. You don't have to pay for some types of advertising on social media, so you might decide to run a social media campaign.

**Social Media Campaign**

What is a social media campaign? When you want to engage people in your social media, to get noticed or to add more followers or connections, you might decide to run a social media campaign. An example would be to choose a title or a theme and write several posts ready to go out to your social media channels for your followers to engage in. By choosing a theme you keep all your posts roughly about the same thing until the end of the campaign. This makes it easier for people to engage and join in with the conversation as they can see what has gone before.

If it is a subject in which they are interested (which goes back to what your avatar is interested in), you will find people will connect with what you have to say. You can schedule posts to go out at a particular time, write blogs and updates connected to your theme in advance. You may also be looking at what is already out there in social media and share that, if it fits with what you want to say.

Campaigns can be run for as long as you like; you may choose to do one over several weeks or just one week or even one day, if it fits in with what you want to share. It's good to keep an eye on what is happening in the world calendar too, so that you can join in with the wider conversation about particular events and use this to share to your own audience. Innovative, catchy titles work best for your blogs and posts, if you can think of them.

To find out if your marketing strategy is working you should track the success of your campaigns. Most social media platforms have ways in which you can track how many people have read your posts, how many engaged with them (answered or joined in) and the reach, for example, if they shared your post to others. This will help to see if you are engaging the right type of comment and person.

If you are not engaging with people as much as you want, you may need to adjust what you are putting out there. It could be that your 'voice' is not authentic (it doesn't sound like you), or that your title is not attention grabbing, or that you have put this out on a day when something else equally important was happening, so your post(s) got lost. All these things will help you to understand better next time you run a campaign, so it's a very useful exercise to monitor and track.

When you have people engaged you can decide the next step you wish to take with them. Will you send them targeted emails about something they are interested in? Will you have a call to action, for example, a 'sign up here for …', etc, etc. Marketing yourself is a huge area and one on which you could spend lots of time. I suggest you follow this basic plan until you find your feet but depending on your situation, you may want to learn more about marketing, so head to the internet and fill your boots.

**Branding**

Branding and marketing are often put together but are distinctly different. When we talk about branding, we are talking about promoting a product, service or yourself, through advertising with a distinctive design.

When I set up a business from an incubator in Manchester, we had lots of help with branding. Your brand is your face to the world and should permeate all that you do. Particularly when you are setting up a business, you need to think about how you want the world to see you (as a person who is head of this business).

This goes back to thinking about your vision and values, which is why we have covered them already. Your brand and that of your business should align with what you are doing or want to do. For example, if you want to be known as an expert in something, you will work hard to gain qualifications, accolades, testimonials in that area to prove to the outside world that you are worthy of that expertise.

It would go against the alignment of your business if you then started to go off at a tangent, particularly with something that doesn't fit in with what people expect you to be talking about. So, if you are an expert in colour correction for hair and well known for this in your business, it would seem odd if you then started to talk about wine tasting, unless it was in a social sense, as this would confuse people. You might also be in danger of diluting your message.

> **TIP**
> Make everything you do fit in with who you want to be known as. Stick to your brand.

**Brand stories**

We were encouraged in our early-stage businesses at the incubator, to develop our brand stories (the story of your business). In an established business there are stories and ways of doing things, characters past and present to discuss. As part of a new person's induction into the business, they are told about some of these stories and it all goes to help them feel more part of the team.

A new business like yours does not have that history to work with but you can start to develop it from day one. I recommend that you document in some way your business story, what made you start up, why certain things are important to you and so on. This is a useful exercise in itself as a memory jogger but also starts to build up your brand.

You can use this on your website in the 'about us' page, where you talk about the business and the reason for setting it up and your part in it. This ongoing piece of work does two things for you, firstly it serves as a record which you will love going through in the future when this start up process is a distant memory, and secondly, it becomes part of your story, which in turn is part of your branding.

***On your own***
Find somewhere (online or in a notebook) to write about how you started the business and why. Continually add to it like a diary of your business to be used for other purposes in the future.

**People buy from people**
Have you ever heard that saying? What it essentially means is that people, in general, trust other people. That is why getting a review or testimonial is so important. If someone trusts you and your product and they share that information with others, this can be a great way to market your business and to build up your brand. In the olden days we would call this word of mouth and I suppose it's no different now, it's just that we tend to use online platforms to write our comments as well as mentioning our experiences to friends. When looking at a new product do you tend to look at the reviews of the product before making a purchase? Such is the power of the review.

**Happy to Share**
You will need to decide what you are happy to share with the world. This is something I personally find difficult to come to terms with, as I am a very private person. But to give some of yourself to your business you will need to share things. When I look at social media profiles, I have a rule that I don't engage with anyone who I cannot see a picture of. It's just that I like to know I am (hopefully!), dealing with a human being. Another is to keep it professional. I re-read my posts and replies to make sure that I am coming across as I would want to be and that nothing said is ambiguous or unkind.

I'm not interested in criticising people either. I think it's best not to engage with anyone who is not fitting into my brand ethos. This is very important. I have had to delete some people from my social media accounts as they are posting things which come onto my pages. I do not want to be associated with certain kinds of posts, so I don't keep them as contacts or friends. I'm not talking about personal views, for example, political, I'm talking about negative views about wider issues, like race or gender.

Customers and clients can search social media to find out about people. I wouldn't want them to think that I thought some of the 'skewed' views out there had got my endorsement. I suppose what I am saying is be careful to monitor your own social presence to ensure your brand message is consistent and take swift action to put things right if not. Your business and branding are too precious to be ruined by someone else's views.

Messages that you are happy to share can be a valuable way for customers to see your brand personality. Each time you put something onto your website or social media, you are building your brand, so make sure it is all aligned. Also, I believe it is important to be yourself. Being authentic will win people's trust and as we know, people buy from people, so trust is quite important.

If you try to write or act differently from the way you usually do, you will be sussed out as a fraud and lose trust. People are very perceptive and will know if you are being yourself or trying to be something else. In addition, this is your voice and that of your business. Can you imagine having to speak in a voice that you don't feel comfortable with for the length of your business life, online and in person?

**TIP**
Be authentically you. Don't try to be someone else, no matter how much you think it would be good for business. It won't. The world will suss you out.

**Overshare is overkill**

Be aware that if you are sharing information online you don't need to tell everyone everything. If, for example, you run a breakfast bar café as your business, then yes, by all means share what you had for breakfast. However, if your business is nothing to do with breakfasts, why would your clients be interested in what you had for yours? It would only serve to weaken your exposure as a businessperson if you started to share such things.

Similarly, if you go bowling with a group of colleagues, the photos may not be appropriate for sharing on your business profile. Unless of course this was a treat for your team having hit their targets, or to settle in a new member of staff. I think you get the idea. Share with purpose or not at all.

**Branding of the business**

This is what most people think of as branding. This is where you consider the colours you use, the type set and fonts in your literature. There is lots of information out there on the use of colour and people's perception of, and reaction to it. You can use this to your advantage to portray how you wish to be known. Some colours and fonts lend themselves to being honest and trustworthy, or perhaps you want to be seen as being a bit more fun in your business.

At this early stage the choice is yours but think carefully about colour in your business. You can use the piece you did on values earlier to help make your decisions about how you want to be viewed by the world. If you make a mistake you will have to re-brand (change the fonts, style, colours, etc. of your promotional material) and this might prove costly, so a little thought at the start may get you to the right place.

**Your values and your business**

What is important to you? We have already talked about your values aligning with your business and your personality. What personality traits do you want to be associated with?

When you meet someone for the first time sometimes you just 'click' which may be because you have a lot in common, but it is also highly likely that you share some similar core values. In a business, you should consider who gets involved and speaks your message and whether their values align with yours.

Colleagues can be trained in systems or mechanical procedures, as in the chapters on planning or paperwork, but it is very difficult to work alongside someone who does not share your core values. Luckily for you, you don't have to. It is your business and one of the beauties of this is you get to choose who you associate with (to a point). If you like to surround yourself with people with a positive outlook then do that, if you prefer thoughtful, problem solving people in your business, put them in. We will talk more about employees and how to find the right person in the next chapter, but it is up to you who you work with, so make sure you align with someone who shares your values.

**Honesty is the best policy**

I had a situation in one of my businesses where a member of staff was stealing time from us. They did this by signing themselves out when they weren't actually working and therefore gained more hours pay. This came to light via another staff member letting us know what was happening.

One of my core values in my businesses is honesty. I talk about this at interview so that everyone is clear that I would rather have honesty, even if it means admitting we have a problem.

The member of staff in question had been trusted with the completion of this paperwork. Imagine my disappointment when this was brought to my attention. For us it meant trawling through records to see if there was any truth in it before confronting them.

I wobbled a bit on trusting employees after that, which was completely unfair to the majority of the people who work with me. Needless to say, that person no longer works for us. It's difficult to come back from such a blatant breach and abuse of trust. I thought this person aligned with and understood the importance of my values, business and personal, but I had obviously misjudged them and not made my values clear enough (some personal training issues for me to work with).

Make sure your values are aligned, not only with your business but those who work in it as well. After all, when you are not there, they are representing your company and you, so this needs to be right.

**Branding and your mission statement**

When you set out your business plan, you wrote your business mission statement. Now that you are clear on your values and branding you will need to re-visit it, to make sure it aligns with who or what you want to be. I know it's difficult to write a succinct mission statement, capturing the essence of what you want to say, therefore you should spend some time on it. When you have the mission statement you are looking for, put it on your business plan and onto your website as well and if possible, include a tag line, or extra phrase for impact.

**An example mission statement**

When I first set up my childcare business in 2001, I knew that I needed to set a mission statement which captured what I wanted to achieve. I came up with one which still stands today - 'professional, affordable childcare'. It summed up where I wanted to position the business and we still use the phrase today. I was keen that childcare was affordable for people and I was coming at the business from a professional background, so all good.

A few years later, when considering my branding, I wanted to change the focus onto our customers rather than the business. In essence our customers are the parents of the children who attend our childcare settings, but I wanted to take it right back to the users with something that would speak to the parents as well.

I came up with 'Recommended by Children' as our tag line, which I have protected by trademark, and I still love it. For me it describes the fun the children have when they are with us and parents feel their children are happy in our care.

So, when you put the two together you have:

Professional, affordable childcare – recommended by children. Short sweet and to the point, this phrase has taken me through almost twenty years of being in business because it aligns with my core values and did so right from the beginning.

Don't be concerned if you can't think of a succinct phrase as your mission or tag line yet, there's plenty of time to work something out, which I'm sure you will as you begin to work out what is important for your brand. By switching the focus of my brand over to my intended customers I was able to come up with something from their point of view. You can too. If you haven't got something in mind at the moment, don't try to force it. The right words will come when they are ready.

**Your business logo**

We all know about logos. We see them everywhere. Even small children can recognise logos. A logo is an instant brand recognition tool so it's important to get it right. Most people will need some help in designing their logo and there will be an associated cost. This will be money well spent; if you get a professional to work on your logo it will show and stand the test of time. When designing the logo for your business, think about the colours and how the typeset and font, colour, shapes and patterns will reflect your business.

**How to help your designer**

Unless your business is to do with design, or you have some expertise in this field, do not think that you can design your own logo. Instead, put your ideas together and show it to a designer who will be able to professionalise your design, making the whole thing look fantastic.

Obviously, you are in the best position to understand your business and what you want your logo to convey so if you provide the ideas then the designer has something to work with. When I use designers, I tend to have a bit of an idea plus an open mind (just in case they come up with something much better). I like to look around at logos I like, this may be to do with lettering, colour or spacing, pictures, etc. From a designer's point of view, if you give them plenty of examples of what you like, they can usually see some sort of a pattern in your choices and they start to work from there. There are all sorts of rules and conventions around spacing and what looks good in terms of design which is why you need someone to help you.

I also provide a few images, colours, etc. that I don't like, so that we are clear on the style I want to achieve. Don't worry if the designer comes up with something that you don't like too much at first. Explain to them why you are not keen. A good designer will work with this new information.

I have worked with quite a few designers over the years, particularly to design logos, and I can honestly say that I still love all my past and present logos because they are aligned with each of the business' values and the look we were trying to achieve. Some of my logos are twenty years old, surely that's got to be worth the outlay.

**Marketing and the competition**

Most likely you will not be the only business in your area doing what you do; there will be competition. Competition does not have to be a bad thing; you could use it to your advantage. For example, you often see a lot of car dealers all in one area, next door to each other. This is planned. Car dealers recognise that people don't want to go travelling all over town, park up and look at individual makes of car. People like to have everything conveniently together and may look at a car make that they wouldn't normally consider if they are all in one area.

The car dealers use each other to help them in sales rather than seeing each other as competition. They may all sell cars, but they all sell different cars. So, in general terms, the product is the same but also quite different. This can be an advantage to your marketing plans. Instead of looking at the competition in a negative way, try seeing it as a good thing and whether that can fit into your strategy.

**Research the Competition**

This is why it is so important to distinguish yourself from the rest of the crowd by establishing your Unique Selling Point (USP). What is it that you have got or do that distinguishes you from the competition? If you are not sure at this stage what your USP is, do some research. This is not spying on the competition, it's research. Don't be fooled, as soon as you and your product or service are out there, others will be researching you!

An example of good USP is John Lewis – never knowingly undersold - you know you are going to get a good deal if you shop there. Their USP also serves as their tag line so a double bonus.

How you go about your research will depend on your competition. You will need to recognise and acknowledge that competition exists and will form part of your business plan. If you are organised, you might decide to set up a spreadsheet and look at all the local (and national?) competition;

• What they offer – you can probably find this out by visiting or getting someone else to visit on your behalf, or by checking out their website.
• Location – where have they set up their business (non-online), have they chosen a high street or an out-of-town location? Try to work out why, as this will help when deciding on your own location.
• Their charging strategy – you may be able to see a price list for individual products or do they charge by the hour? If you can see what other people are charging it is easier to pitch your own pricing structure. Remember though that just to undercut the competition is lazy.

**Make what you offer do the talking, not the price.**

• Their marketing strategy, if you can work it out – this sounds like you wouldn't be privy to such things but with a little bit of investigation you will be surprised at what you can see. For example, part of their marketing approach may be to blog on their own website every week or send out a newsletter. You may see that they post on social media platforms regularly and what they post about. They already have a customer base and you do not. Who are these people and where do they go to find out about things?

• Market share- seems difficult to quantify but you can do this in a rudimentary way. If they are the only shop in the town, they probably have 100% of the market share in that town. If there are two similar shops then don't presume they have 50% each; one may have 40%, one 60% and this could be to do with any of the factors we are discussing, for example, better location, more footfall, or a more engaging website if it is online.

• Their USP – this should be obvious when you are doing your research; what are they continually flagging up to their customers about what makes them different. Long gone are the days when it was all based on owner personality, people are looking for more now, switching loyalties when something better comes along. You just have to be better. That's why undercutting on price is such a short term a strategy.

**Working with the competition**

It is better in the long run for you to know all about your competition, you may even be able to work with them if your offering is quite different or if there is space in the market for both of you. You could advise potential customers that the competition will better fit their needs and vice versa, if that is the case. Please remember that the competition is just as interested in you as you are in them.

Sometimes it works well to introduce yourself to them right at the beginning and explain how you are different to their offering and therefore how you can work alongside each other. It is quite a brave ask but if you have researched them and found that you have something quite different, it might be they assume you are copying them and see it as a negative thing.

If you are offering quite different products or services, then they cease to become competition. After all, you may be attending the same meetings in your field or training and networks so you will probably come across them locally.

**Reaching out to the competition**
I once went to visit some local competitors at their premises to introduce myself. They automatically assumed I was there to spy which I found quite amusing. They were far enough away from our premises for them not to be competing for the same customers, but as is often the case in these matters, we do tend to churn around the same employees from business to business over the years.

They panicked when they saw me approaching. They recognised me even though this was my first time meeting them (I told you that other businesses research their competition!). They were very guarded when I introduced myself as being fairly local and wanting to introduce myself. I eventually got invited into their office. The brief meeting was formal and odd and I left feeling that they were really worried by my visit. I didn't realise I had such power!

This company assumed I was negative competition for them, when all I was trying to do was make friends. I can only assume that during their research on me they had found something to worry about in terms of their own business. Because the meeting was so strained, I have not returned to that company. This is of course their loss. With other competitors that I introduced myself to on the same day and much closer in location than them, we have enjoyed sharing training and other initiatives, bringing down the costs for both of us.

**Chapter Takeaways**
Developing a marketing plan is similar to developing your business plan; start with the end in mind. Deciding on what you want your outcomes to be helps you to focus on what to include in your plan. Considering your target market at a detailed level will help to understand who your best customers are and where to find them.

By considering ROI, rather than cost, in your marketing campaigns you will see the value of spending money on getting the right customers. Use the 5-star marketing plan to help you to get your marketing thoughts and plans in place.

Branding permeates all that your business stands for so should be carefully thought out. Be continually mindful to align your branding with your business.

**Call to action**

Spend time deciding on your avatar
Use the 5-star marketing plan to develop ways of getting out to market
Develop a social media plan and campaigns
Think carefully about how to brand your business
Competition can be positive
Everything should be aligned to your business and personal values

*"People will forget what you said, people will forget what you did, but people will never forget how you made them feel."*

*Maya Angelou*

# Chapter Seven: Staff

For some of you this may be a chapter too far, in that you are not going to start a business where you need staff. However, if like me you started a business where you are not allowed to work alone due to regulations, then there is no choice. I also include this chapter for completeness so you can think about what having a team would be like.

**Do you need Employees?**
As I don't know which type of business you are setting up, I am ending the book with employing people. You may already know that you will not be needing or using others to assist you. Your alternatives are:

- **Do everything yourself**

  By choosing this option you will have to learn a lot of new business regulations and procedures, as well as the practical side of your particular business (which you're probably up to speed with already). This is quite a task to take on but with time, patience and guidance you should be able to do this.
- **Outsource some of the business roles**

  List the main tasks within your business, then decide which ones you will need to outsource, either regularly or on an ad hoc basis. This allows you to concentrate on doing the tasks you know how to do well, leaving the experts to do the rest. This will, however, impact on running costs, affecting your break-even and profit margin.

- **Employ contractors who look after their own employment rights**

  I thought I would put this one in here, as we have not talked about using agency staff or contractors yet. This is when you want a specific task or job doing and you pay someone for the whole job. You don't employ them directly, so you don't get involved in their tax and national insurance, just like employing a plumber to come to your house to fix a leaky tap. He comes and gives you a quote which includes his time, expertise, parts and VAT, if applicable. You pay the figure at the bottom of the invoice and the job is done. From the plumber's point of view, he has to make sure he pays all tax due, etc. but this is not a concern to you, as you have paid for the whole job. An agency works in a similar way; if you need a staff member for two days and call an agency, they supply the staff member, you pay the agency and the agency pays the member of staff. Your contract is with the agency, not the temporary staff member.
- **Take staff on in your business.**

  This means you have the responsibility of employing people, which we will talk about in the following sections.

**To Employ or not to Employ**

In my childcare business I had to take on employees straight away, as the regulations do not allow you to work alone with children in a care setting. This meant that from the very first minute of opening my business I was not only doing something new by having a business, I also became an employer.

A few years later, I set up a different business, using an online system with no requirement for employees. However, as that business developed, additional help was required to run it efficiently, so we had to take someone on part time.

**Something To Think About**

**Employing people in your business**
For me, the biggest impact of employing people is the responsibility. If having responsibility for others is a major issue for you, then employing people may be conflicting for you and you may need to seek out other business opportunities or look at ways that you can run your business without employing people. Some of those responsibilities include wages, PAYE, pensions, employment rights, disputes, redundancy, suitability and insurance. This is not an exhaustive list and it's not here to frighten you, but it does need consideration.

There is a lot to taking on employees, so we are going to go through the reality of employing people in this chapter. You may decide, after reading this, that employing someone is not for you at the moment and that's ok. If you are unsure or uncomfortable, use an outside agency to employ people for you. There will, of course, be a cost implication but an agency will ensure that you are on the right side of the law.

If you have to take someone on, you will discover that employing people is all about procedure and doing things correctly, to protect your staff member and yourself. Employing people can't be that bad, or no-one would be employed! Most of what you are about to read and learn in this chapter can be outsourced, so if you feel that you want to jump off at any time, you are able to do so. If, however, you recognise that many a good business is built on a strong team then stick with it. By learning about employing people, you are in control of who you take on to help your business and when you do that.

**Who can help?**
There is help out there when you are employing someone for the first time to resolve queries and questions. I suggest you get ahead of the game with employment rights and related issues. As an employer, you have direct access to an organisation called

ACAS, which stands for the Advisory, Conciliation and Arbitration Service. The role of ACAS is to help both employers and employees if they have a query about Employment Law. This service is free and confidential. Many think ACAS is just there on behalf of employees, to take employers to tribunal over an employment dispute. It is true this is one of their roles. However, they are mainly there to advise both employees and employers on what the law states in relation to employment and to give advice based on that.

In addition, your insurance company policy may include access to legal advice, so it's worth checking that as well. We have legal advice included with our insurance policy; the insurance company outsource this to a local solicitor's Employment Law department. This usually means that after the introduction from the insurance company, you deal directly with the solicitor. Alternatively, you may want to use an Employment Law company. They will charge a monthly fee for their services, depending on how many staff you have. However, they will manage all your HR functions and be on the end of the phone for advice on any employment issue.

**Clarity, Consequences and Consistency**

When employing someone for the first time, you should be mindful of your values and how you want to be perceived. The bottom line is to aim to be fair in your dealings with staff and the expectations you have of them. By treating employees well, you will develop a reputation for fairness which will help when you want to recruit again. Later in this chapter we will go through recruitment in detail.

When setting up your staff contracts, job descriptions, and induction procedures you will need to have clarity of purpose. By knowing what you want the staff member to achieve you will both be clear on the expectations. As a result, you will be able to decide on the consequences for non-compliance with the behaviours you want.

For example, if you have a probation period of a few months;

• what happens at the end of this period?
• what are the consequences for the employee if they pass or fail the probationary period?
• who is judging this?
• what are the benchmarks?
• how can the employee be supported if you, or they, feel they are not going to hit certain targets?

By outlining the consequences, positive and negative, it means everyone is clear about what happens next. Finally, you need to be consistent in your approach. It is important that you treat all employees in the same way. If you treat an individual differently, other employees will have recourse to question this and possibly take further action against you, depending on what the inconsistency entails.

This is why it is important to have policies in place before you start to recruit. Your policy should outline the route you are expected to follow in your own procedures and will be linked to your contracts, discipline and grievance policies. By having policies in place before you need them you stay ahead of the game. This will, in turn, give you confidence in dealing with employing people.

**A word about staff relationships**

The relationship between employer and employee is a professional one and should always remain so. This is an area which can be a little hazy, particularly for first time employers (or managers come to that), who think that they have to be best friends with their employees to show they are friendly and that they care. Remember, they work for you, not the other way around. Don't let personal relationships get in the way of professionalism in the workplace. You can be friendly but remember that at some point you may have to discipline this person and your relationship could be compromised if you are too close to them.

Think carefully about employing family and friends for the same reason. You may have a situation where you have to act in a professional manner which may be seen by your friend or family member as unfriendly. You may lose a friend or an employee due to this kind of situation. Better to steer clear of an awkward situation before it has the chance to occur. Similarly, if you dislike someone on a personal level you must not let this affect your working relationship. That is why it is better to recruit your own staff, if possible, so you know they fit in with your values and there is less likelihood of problems in the future.

**Outsourcing - advantages and disadvantages**

As previously mentioned, there are companies that can take on all your employment needs. They will, for a fee, advertise your post, shortlist and interview candidates, set up employment contracts and anything else required to do with recruitment. There are even companies that will go and find them, i.e. headhunt the candidates for you as well. If you would like to take advantage of the services offered by these companies, search on Google for recruitment and you will probably find someone reputable locally.

A word of warning about using these companies though. Firstly, the costs can be quite prohibitive, as they are putting a lot of effort into recruiting staff for you and as this is their business, they will want to make it worth their while. Secondly, you would need to make sure that your brief about exactly what you want for your recruit is very explicit. They can only work with the details you give them. Thirdly, and this goes back to your values, if you don't recruit the person yourself, there may be a mismatch between your values and their values.

The advantages of using an agency for recruitment is that you will not have to lift a finger; they will do it all. In addition, you may be offered an ongoing Human Resources (HR) package, covering all your staffing needs from when they are appointed. If this is the case, they will come into your company to check that all your staffing policies and procedures align and that the employment contracts are safe for you and employees. If there is a problem, question or dispute, you contact them; they then tell you exactly how to deal with it. Usually, they do not come to your company in person but offer step by step advice by telephone and email for you to follow. It is still your staff member and still your business, but this kind of handholding can offer peace of mind in an uncertain area of your business.

Apart from the initial and ongoing monthly costs, some business owners feel a lack of control by using an outside company. Their rules are quite strict; they have to be. You may negate the contract with them by not following their advice, not getting in touch, or waiting too long when a situation is developing to inform them. An outside company will always be a little removed from your team and your business because they are not in it on a daily basis. It could also be seen as a bit cold, as it takes away the human side of give and take with staffing. In addition, it is harder for outside agencies to take into consideration any mitigating circumstances, whereas you know about those as you are with your employees every day. It is, however, fair.

Agencies and companies that deal with all your HR and staffing needs can often use scaremonger tactics to enrol you in their programme, such as talking about times when other companies have been taken to tribunal by their employees who won huge pay-outs. I have been along to these talks and the stories *are* scary; they do make you worried that every one of your employees will take you to the cleaners financially. However, for every scare story, there are more tales of people being successfully employed for long periods of time. It's a question of comfort and balance. Do what you feel comfortable with but don't forget that the balance of probabilities suggest that you will not get into problems by recruiting people, if you do things properly, with or without outside help.

**Outsourcing only some of the workload**

Some roles can be outsourced and it is up to you to decide which. If you are choosing to use an agency to take on your HR as discussed above, you may decide there are some things you want them to do and others you don't. That's fine; get them to do the tasks you think you will find most challenging and have a go at the rest yourself.

You don't have to use one company to fulfil all your needs. You could separate the tasks out. For example, in my business we prepare all the payroll and wage information, then pass it on to an outsourced company who submit the figures we have given them to HMRC. We rely on them for advice on certain staffing issues to do with wages, pensions, statutory sickness and parental leave. We have considered, many times, finishing the job off ourselves and hiring someone in-house to send the wages through an online programme like SAGE but have never got around to this. This would mean we would have full responsibility for all the wages, but I prefer to pay someone else to take that responsibility. Don't forget that any mistakes they make may reflect badly on you and your company as employees automatically assume that it is *your* mistake.

Training is another area that can be outsourced, particularly if you are short on time. However, there will be certain types of training that you will want to do yourself, or at least in-house and that's understandable, like for example induction of new staff. Other types of training may be beyond your skill or confidence level, for example we have to outsource first aid training as this is a specialist area.

Some business owners outsource their financial auditing to either an accountant or a bookkeeper. I prefer to keep this job to myself for the simple reason that I like to know my numbers. When you are reconciling bank accounts on a regular basis, you are in a position to see what is going on really quickly, to spot trends and also deal with any potential worries. I let the accountants complete the audited accounts at the end of the year though, to pass on to HMRC.

**Victims of fraud**

We have been the victims of fraud several times over the years through our business bank accounts. Because I access and reconcile my accounts most days, I have been able to respond quickly when we have fallen victim to a fraudulent attack. Once, someone got into our bank account and set themselves up as one of my payees. At the time I was paying around 60-70 people, all on the same day.

The fraudster paid themselves on the same (pay) day from our account. They gave themselves around three times the highest wage that I had ever paid, so the fraud stood out quite visibly. As soon as it happened, I contacted the bank and they were able to see it was a fraudulent transaction. The bank refunded the money into our account, but I think the fraudster got away with it. Perhaps he or she would have taken money again the next day if I had not been so quick to react and report what I had seen. That is one reason why I like to be on the numbers daily.

Within your company, financial control could be given to someone else. Needless to say, this would have to be a trusted member of staff and you might consider having a police background check done prior to giving them access to your bank accounts. This type of role is notoriously open to abuse, through theft, massaging the figures, paying out extra and generally dipping into funds. There is no easy answer to this. If you are not going to do this yourself you will have to trust someone else to do it, whether this be a company or a dedicated member of staff in your company. I always trust everyone to start with, but I do watch carefully!

***On Your Own***
Make a list of the tasks and jobs you are considering outsourcing and make some enquiries as to cost, timing, etc., to see if this could be an option for you.

**Employing People**

**Role map**
You need to start thinking big for your business. Even if you are not taking on employees yet, it is a good idea to decide on the roles that will be inside your business as it grows. You may find you are the one who fulfils all those roles for the moment, but as your business gets bigger you may outsource tasks, or take on employees to fill the roles. Map out the business in terms of

staffing requirements and attach a job description to each role. To start with make it quite simple and then fill in the gaps.
It may mean there are fifteen roles in the business, and you fulfil 14 of them and outsource one, and that's ok. As the business grows you will change the role map to either include specific people or outsource specific roles. When you are starting out in business, you really do have to be the Jack or Jill of all trades.

***On Your Own***
Make your own Role Map for your business.

**Job descriptions**
What is a job description and what it is for? Why do we need one?
A job description is useful in setting out the roles and responsibilities of the job. When you are recruiting, it's a good idea to send out a job description to prospective candidates so they can see if the job is suitable for them. This gives them an insight into the role, prior to applying. Alongside that I always send a person specification as well.

The person spec tells the prospective candidate what sort of person you expect to be applying for this role, including qualifications and skills. Some employers write by the side of the list whether it is essential or desirable, so each candidate gets an idea of what is acceptable. This does two things. Firstly, you are allowing candidates to self-select. If they don't like the look of your job description or can't fit into your person specification, they probably won't apply. This is a great way to save time for both you and them. Secondly, they already know what is expected of them in terms of their role and responsibilities when it comes to their induction.

It's about thinking bigger than the business currently is which is exciting. When you are just starting out, you will want to tweak job roles as you do them (on your own) to make sure you get the role fulfilled in the way you want it done. This may be fluid as you develop the business and realise you need to create more positions or can consolidate smaller roles into making a complete role and get someone in post.

**Qualifications versus experience**

Having decided you need to employ someone, you will need to look at their qualifications and experience for the role you are offering. It may be that a certain qualification is essential in your line of work. If it is, don't compromise. What is the point in you taking someone on because they are 'nice', when they do not fulfil what you need in the role? Most people are on their best behaviour when they come for interview; people tend to make an effort with cleanliness and clothes to give you a good impression.

I am keen on candidates who show respect by turning up for interview on time and well presented. As you can imagine, having an employment rich business, I have had my fair share of interviews with prospective candidates over the years and I've probably seen it all! But perhaps those tales are for another time!

You will need to make a judgement about who you employ; if this is based on qualifications, make sure you see the originals. Anyone can write about numerous qualifications on a C.V. but you will need to see the actual qualification if you decide to employ this person, then take a scan or photo of the qualification for their file. This is why you need to see their photographic identification as well.

You may, however, be searching for someone who has experience in a certain area, whether this be technical experience or actual experience of doing a particular task or role. Some people don't have qualifications, but their experience can be proven by asking for references, and they may be just what you are looking for. If you don't need the actual qualification, don't get hung up on it if you get a great candidate without the paperwork but with the right background.

You may find that someone is qualified, but their lack of experience makes it difficult as they need training. Who will do this? You therefore need to decide on the ideal candidate and then be flexible. Remember, you may not get what you are looking for, so may have to compromise, do without or re-start the recruitment process. Or you could offer a temporary trial or short-term contract initially, to make sure the person is a good fit.

**Recruitment**

Another minefield is recruitment. You will need to abide by the rules and regulations of Employment Law. This is an area that you might choose to outsource, bearing in mind what was discussed earlier about employing people who share your values, or you can have a go yourself. Recruitment agencies will charge to help you appoint someone and may also have ongoing costs, so beware!

Taking people on into your business can be a very rewarding experience. You are now at the point where you need some additional help to run your business. What a metaphorical pat on the back that is! If you know the right steps to take, you can set out a plan for recruitment. Let's decide you need to recruit one member of staff; by following the Ten Step Plan to Recruitment, you can get there.

**The Ten Step Plan to Recruitment**

**Step One - Start with the end in mind.**

I knew that this would come in handy when I wrote it at the beginning of the book. In this case, what you need to look at is when you want your new employee to start. However, a word of warning, don't put the decision to employ someone off until you are desperate and need someone straight away, as that will compromise you and the recruitment process. As with most things in business, if you know when your end date is, it's easier to plan how to get there in a timely manner.

**Step Two - Decide on the role to be filled**

That sounds a bit obvious but there is no point in just saying you would like an admin person. You need to think about the actual role they will fulfil, the hours you want them to work (and whether you are flexible about this), where you want them to work and on which particular tasks. You are setting out a job description for the role. If you already have one (from when you created your Role Map) check this is still exactly what you want. This is the time you can make the job role fit exactly what you want so, for example, if you want the new person to work across lunchtime, as you get lots of calls then, you are able to set the hours now. Anyone who does not want to do those hours will not apply for your job, so no time is wasted.

**Step Three - Decide on your person specification.**
We talked before about deciding what is essential for your post and what is desirable. Take a look at the new job description and decide what the person will need to be able to do to fulfil that role. If it is a requirement that they have a qualification in something, state it as an essential. If you want them to work evenings or weekends mention this now. If you need someone with a certain level of financial ability, would this be through a qualification, for example a GCSE, or does the work require a higher level of understanding?
You will be sending out both the job description and the person spec to everyone who applies, so you will need to give them a clue as to how they will prove the information. If, for example, you need someone with GCSE Maths and English, you can request that they bring along their certificates to the interview.

When you send the job description and person spec out to prospective candidates is up to you. You may have included both in the application pack on your website or you could email it to the successful applicants. You just need to remember that at every stage, with each additional piece of information, candidates will self-select and you will lose some, and that's fine. You don't want to be wasting anyone's time, including your own. Better for them to drop out of the selection process sooner rather than later.

**Step Four - The job advert**
You will need to write a job advert for this new role and post it on a job vacancies website or space, for example, Indeed.

Writing the job advert is not a difficult task once you have completed the job description and person spec, as you know exactly what you are looking for. You may need to put the salary or wage onto the job advert, in addition to hours, basic job role and where the post is going to be based. You don't have to write everything on the job advert, but you must write enough about the job to allow a person to decide whether or not they want to apply. When you have written your advert, check it through to make sure that it's not ambiguous, as you don't want people ringing you to ask questions, e.g. is it full time or where is it based, etc. Your job advert should include details of how the candidates can apply to you. Do you want them to write you a letter, include their C.V. or download an application from your website? What is the closing date for the job? Try to give at least two weeks minimum for people to apply.

**TIP**
You must make sure your advert is not discriminatory in any way. For example, you cannot advertise for an 18-year-old school leaver as this is seen as age discrimination, so keep your advert general. If in doubt, have a look at the ACAS website or give them a call to make sure you are on the right side of the law.

**Step Five - Sorting through the applicants**

When you get to the closing date, hopefully you will have some applicants. How many applicants you get depends on the type of role it is. When we recently advertised for a part time administrator, we had over 120 applicants. However, this may not be the case for your job which is why there is a process to go through.

To help you sort out who you would like to take through to the next stage of the process, I suggest you make two piles. One is 'no' and one is 'maybe'. On the 'no' pile you might put people who do not have the essential qualification they need, or if you are looking for experience, they don't have it. You need to have a valid reason for saying no. This cannot be anything like 'they live too far away', as you don't know their circumstances and if they have applied to you, the distance is *their* issue. I always send a brief rejection email to the no's (but not yet, in case I need to make sure I've not been too hasty!). This may say something along the lines of they have been unsuccessful at this stage. Short and sweet but courteous. The 'maybe' pile will need to be sifted more carefully, again sending out a brief email to those who are unsuccessful.

Ideally you will end up with a small pile of candidates who meet the criteria you set out in the person spec and job description.

**Step Six - Invitation to interview**

You now have some candidates you would like to interview. When you wrote the job advert, you indicated both closing date and the expected interview date(s), so hopefully the interviewees will be available. You will need to send them a letter or email with the time, date and place they are to be interviewed. You should allow enough time to interview each candidate before seeing the next one, so stagger the interviews. Don't forget you will need to allow a comfort break for yourself and anyone else interviewing. If you have not already done so, make sure the candidate has seen the job description and person spec, so they know the rough format of the interview and can prepare. Also, you should ask the candidate to bring along their relevant qualifications and some form of identification. You will need to know that they are who they say they are!

**Step Seven - Who will interview?**

You will, is the obvious answer. However, you also need someone with you if possible, to balance the interview and to make sure that you are being fair, in addition to you having someone you trust to support you. Sometimes you have a panel of people interviewing who all come from different sections of the business, but I am guessing you are not going to be at that stage yet, so you will have to go with what you have got.

**Step Eight - The interview Questions**

What are you going to ask the candidates? And in what order? It's a good idea to start with an easy question to relax them into the interview. I recommend you have a list of prepared questions, and the sort of answers you are looking for. For example, if you want to know what they know about a certain industry issue, ask them something like, 'Tell me what you know about…'. This is an open-ended question and allows them to show their knowledge and experience of the issue.

Meanwhile, you will have a list of words at the side of your question sheet that you would expect the candidate to mention. You can tick these off as they do and even prompt a little if they forget any. On your question sheet you would indicate that you had to prompt. I think it's fine to help candidates out a bit in an interview as long as you are consistent with everyone. Sometimes, they have just forgotten something, perhaps due to nerves, and sometimes they don't know, and this will be obvious. If someone doesn't know something even after a prompt, I look at finishing the question and moving on usually by saying thank you (for their answer). You will not know until you get to the end of all the interviews if your question was at fault, so always bear this in mind, particularly if you've not asked these questions before.

Make notes throughout the interview so you can refer to them in the next step. At the end of the interview, thank the candidate for coming, ask if they have any questions to ask you and let them know what happens next. For example, 'We expect to make a decision by the end of the week and will be contacting candidates by email.'

**Step Nine - After the interviews**

When the interviews are over, you get a chance to discuss each candidate, their merits and suitability for the role on offer. This is why you will need your notes. If you have been interviewing all day you will need help to remember which candidate said what. I find it useful to write down anything personal or unusual they said, as this helps me to remember the candidate later. In theory, this stage should be easy as you have already decided on your criteria and person specification. If there is more than one candidate with all the requirements, this is when it starts to get more difficult.

I always look at why we would choose that candidate but also why we wouldn't. We offered a job recently with specific and set hours. The first candidate had everything we wanted except she wanted to change the hours we had set. This was our reason for not taking her on. It could have worked the other way; if she had all the criteria and seemed to be the best candidate, we might have looked at changing the hours. Therefore, in terms of getting the best candidate, you may have to be a bit flexible.

I can't tell you which person will be the best for your business, but you will know, and that is why you have someone else with you, if possible, to share the decision making.

**Step Ten - Informing the candidates**

Unless you are recruiting for a large team, some people will be disappointed that they didn't get chosen to work with you. When you have decided who the lucky person will be, you need to tell them. I suggest you have someone on your list in reserve, if your first choice turns you down. I also suggest you inform the successful candidate first, to make sure they accept the job. I like to get this in writing from them, so a simple email is fine. They will then begin your new employee process, which we will cover later. You are now able to let the other candidates know they have been unsuccessful.

I always say they have been unsuccessful on this occasion. They were successful in gaining an interview, it's just that they weren't the best fit for your company at the moment.
You may be asked by unsuccessful candidates why they didn't get the job. This is where your notes come in handy. If someone was unable to answer certain questions and needed too much prompting on an essential issue, it could indicate a lack of knowledge, or a lack of experience. That is why, in step eight, you were already thinking about this in your questioning. Don't be drawn into lengthy discussions about why candidates didn't get the job. Let them know they were unsuccessful and stop there

unless they ask. If they ask, you can always indicate how the successful person was more experienced or qualified.

The last word on selection is that you don't have to choose a candidate at all. If no-one is suitable feel free not to appoint. Just because you have gone to the trouble of organising and setting up the interviews doesn't mean you will find the right person for the job. If your gut feeling says don't appoint, then don't; you will possibly regret it if you feel under pressure to appoint. Taking on staff should be seen as a long-term commitment and therefore one which is important to get right. We still have people in our businesses who have been with us for over 17 years.

**References and identification**

You remember that at step six I suggested that you ask the candidates to bring along identification with them. This is so you can check their ID and also their right to work in the UK. If your candidate is a foreign national, they will have documentation stating they have the right to work in the UK, which you are responsible for checking.

Depending on your business, you may want to take up references before the interview or after the interview, either is fine.

**A reference or a testimonial?**

Some candidates bring along (what they call) references to the interview. These are not references, they are testimonials. They are usually very positive about the candidate and that is why the candidate wants you to see them. They are not however, a reference. A reference is something which you request from a former employer, trusted professional or friend in the case of personal references and it is specifically for that person's ability to do your specific job.

You can send out the job description and person spec to a potential referee. Hopefully, they will reply, having given due consideration to the candidate's abilities to fulfil the role you are offering, alongside other things like punctuality, ability to work in a team, etc.

A testimonial brought along to the interview cannot be job specific. It can only be general. It may have been written some time ago, when the candidate left someone else's employment. You could write to the author of the testimonial to see if they have written it and if the job you have on offer would be suitable for the candidate but taking a testimonial as a reference is poor practice.
I always check references to make sure the writer did, indeed, write the reference (stranger things have happened!). This might be a quick call to the referee. If they are genuine, they won't mind you double checking this information.

**Your responsibilities towards employees**
When you have employees in your organisation, you have certain responsibilities towards them which you should adhere to.

**Induction**
After their appointment, they should have a period of induction into their new role. On the first day, you must go through any health and safety requirements for example, what to do in the event of a fire, where the toilets are, how long and where to take any breaks, where smoking is allowed (most likely off the premises) and so on. Show them where they are expected to work, if applicable, who is their line manager and who is available to new staff members for questions and training. Over a set period of time you are expected (or someone on your behalf), to train them in their role and to give them feedback so they know how they are doing. They may be on a probationary period with your company and your expectations will need to be clear.

**Wages, contracts and paperwork**
You should create a staff file (preferably online), to store all information regarding their interview, appointment and their job description. Going forward, the file will also contain information about appraisals, disciplinary records and meetings that you have with the staff member. It will also contain their contract of employment, (the new employee needs a copy of this within 6 weeks of starting with you), information about salary or wages

and who to contact in an emergency. You should set them up on your bank account for online payments and on your wages system. You will need their full name, address, NI number, marital status, whether they have another job and if possible, their tax code, although this will be sent from HMRC. It is important to inform HMRC that you have a new employee, as you will be responsible for paying their tax and national insurance, pension contribution, statutory sick and parental leave payments. It sounds like a lot but there are computer programmes which do all of this and the whole job of paying someone could be outsourced if you prefer and can afford it.

**Training and well-being**

You will, of course, need to train your new employee to your company rules, giving them all the information they need to do their job well. You may have to include additional (outside) training as well. New staff should familiarise themselves with your company policies, including holiday entitlement and how to ring in sick.

**TIP**

We ask new staff to read policies and to sign to say they have read and understood them. It is then on record (in their file), that they understand how things operate and their role, which may be useful in any future disputes.

**Chapter Takeaways**

Your new employee will need ongoing support in understanding your expectations linked to the job description. You should make it easy for them to succeed in their new role. Staff well-being is quite high on an employer's agenda and you may want to have a policy in place. By offering a supportive network within the company and beyond, you will be fulfilling your employer obligations to look after your staff. You will also have happy staff and happy staff equals happy customers. Win-win.

For many, the fact you have staff working with you probably means your business has grown to need others within it, which of course is a positive thing. Taking on employees is a huge responsibility but has many rewards. It can give you the opportunity to work *on* your business and not *in* it all the time. This allows you 'thinking' time, which helps you to develop your business further.

**Call to action**

Decide if you need to take on employees, and if you do,
Prepare well in advance
Make sure you are level-headed about who you need in your business
Beware of employing family and friends
Take your responsibility seriously

*"Begin with the end in mind"*

*Stephen Covey*

# Is this the end you had in mind?

This book was written to help you decide whether being an entrepreneur and starting your own business was for you. We started with deciding on the suitability of you as a business owner and of your business idea. You need to consider your current and expected qualifications and whether they make you suitable to run a business. Is the business you have chosen suitable for you, your area and the market?

You need to think about what is already out there in terms of competition and how you can differentiate yourself through your USP. You need to consider your time commitments, how much time you currently have to run a business or how much are you hoping to have in the future to devote to your new venture? You were also encouraged to put a contingency plan in place, bearing in mind over-optimism.

You may have already decided what you want from a business, for example time, money, status or autonomy and as you know, planning is key. Planning for your business starts with considering your business structure and opening a bank account in your business name.

Throughout the book you have been encouraged to think about the end rather than where you are now, which is right at the beginning. This is good business practice as it helps you to know (and plan for) where you are heading.

Your business plan will help to
• focus your ideas,

• set your aims and goals,
• identify potential problems (through your SWOT analysis), and
• measure your progress.

Your on-going plans break down these aims and goals even further into smaller more manageable chunks. From here your SMART action plans help you to get into the minutiae of your plans, ticking off items from your lists as you go. Clear language helps to identify the exact goal you want to achieve.

You have gained an insight into the importance of working *on* your business as well as *in* your business. Most entrepreneurs find this out for themselves along the way, but you will be equipped with this knowledge from the start, so you are already way ahead of the game.

Chapter Three was devoted to looking at the financial aspect of running your own business, where you learned about breakeven points, set up and running costs. Finding money to source your business can be difficult, particularly as a first time business owner with no track record. Regarding sources of funding with caution will lessen your exposure to risk, for you or anyone else.

Sometimes it is better to go softly, softly when setting up on your own and self-fund. If you take things slowly and continue to earn a wage elsewhere you are not putting yourself and your family at unnecessary risk.

It is important to be responsible when it comes to recording financial transactions. You need to do this by using a system so when it comes to income reporting time at the end of the tax year, you have everything in place and don't need to stress. This may be an area that you consider outsourcing.

We discussed whether you needed premises for your new enterprise and if you do, what kind of environment is most suitable for you. Working from home seems like the cheapest way to work, however, it does have its drawbacks and needs careful planning and thought. You need to consider whether your business will be offline or online as both come with a few challenges. The kind and cost of equipment you require needs to be planned for as well, so everything is in one place. Of course, you don't need to buy everything new in order to set up a business; second hand and borrowed equipment will do just fine.

I have tried to outline the kind of paperwork you may require, encouraging you, wherever possible to access resources online. This is for environmental, security and financial reasons. When you run a business, you will need to keep records and know exactly where to find them.

To keep things simple, I have introduced you to the Three Folder System which puts all of your paperwork into just three folders. This makes it easy to find, store and retrieve everything, whether you have a filing cabinet or work within online folders.

Whilst you are at the beginning of your journey it is a really useful exercise to document all your processes and to keep them alongside your policies and procedures in what we call the Office Handbook. This office handbook contains all your business systems with detailed explanations of how to do everything, in one place. This is great if you don't do things very regularly and invaluable when someone else needs to do them.

Part of running your own business is letting people know about what you do so they can buy from you, access your services and so on. You are advised to get a marketing plan in place, including social media, to help you get your business message out there. To do this you will need to be clear about your target audience, who will want to buy from you and where you will find them.

In addition, you need to consider your branding. You already have your USP which aligns to your personal and business goals and so should your branding. Your brand is a lot more than a clever logo in lovely colours. It's a statement put out by you to the world. Hopefully in time, your brand will be recognised, as so many of the larger brands are today. They all started somewhere. Using a designer to help you think about your logo and branding may be an expense, but I honestly think it is worth it. You may carry the same logo for many years so it's worth getting it right at the beginning.

Embrace rather than be afraid of the competition. Competition is good. It can spur you into action or into a joint venture as well as providing you with ideas.

In the last chapter we looked at taking on employees. Although this may be a long way off for you as you are just starting out, I thought I would include it for completeness. As I said, I had to take on employees on my very first day of opening my business, so it could happen to you as well.

The purpose of this book was to give those considering their very first business an understanding of exactly what that could entail. Although there is a lot here to think about it has not been written to put you off, rather to enlighten you. You will be able to take a measured view (no over-optimism, no risk taking) of whether starting a business is for you. I hope you have found it useful.

I have been open about what to expect so you have fewer surprises. Having set up a new business many times, over twenty if you include each site of my childcare business, I know the buzz you get when starting a new business venture. With a little careful thought and planning, there's no reason why you can't join us business owners and entrepreneurs. I wish you every success in your new world.

If you wish to ask any questions, I will do my best to answer them. If you want to tell me how you got on starting your new business, I would be delighted to hear from you. Please contact me through my website - terribourne.com.

Good luck!
Terri

*Your time is limited so don't waste it living someone else's life.*
*Don't be trapped by dogma - which is living with the results of other peoples' thinking.*
*Don't let the noise of other people's opinions drown out your inner voice.*
*And most important, have the courage to follow your heart and intuition"*

*Steve Jobs (founder of Apple)*

Printed in Great Britain
by Amazon

82771405R00088